I'LL GET M

A Farc

by

PHILIP KING

SAMUEL FRENCH

LONDON

NEW YORK   TORONTO   SYDNEY   HOLLYWOOD

ISBN 978-0-573-01533-5

www.samuelfrench-london.co.uk

www.samuelfrench.com

FOR AMATEUR PRODUCTION ENQUIRIES

UNITED KINGDOM AND WORLD EXCLUDING NORTH AMERICA
plays@SamuelFrench-London.co.uk
020 7255 4302/01

Each title is subject to availability from Samuel French,

depending upon country of performance.

I'LL GET MY MAN

First produced by The Southwick Players at the Barn Theatre, Southwick, on the 11th December 1966, with the following cast of characters—

(in order of their appearance)

THE REVEREND ARTHUR HUMPHREY	*Joe Billing*
MRS CARTER	*Ena Collis*
HARRIETTE HUMPHREY	*Sylvia Smithers*
WINIFRED BARRINGTON-LOCKE	*Kay Russell*
PETER ('VENTURE MAN') GRAHAM	*Maurice Pound*
A PHOTOGRAPHER	*Jack Marshall*
JOSEPHINE DE BRISSAC	*Doreen Atkinson*
PIXIE ('I'LL GET MY MAN') POTTER	*Sue Barker*
THE BISHOP OF LAX	*Edmund Andrew*

The Play directed by the Author

Subsequently produced by the Bristol Old Vic Company at the Theatre Royal, Bristol, on the 26th December 1966, with the following cast of characters—

THE REVEREND ARTHUR HUMPHREY	*Larry Noble*
MRS CARTER	*Thelma Barlow*
HARRIETTE HUMPHREY	*Sheila Keith*
WINIFRED BARRINGTON-LOCKE	*Celia Ryder*
PETER ('VENTURE MAN') GRAHAM	*Donald Douglas*
A PHOTOGRAPHER	*Brian Gwaspari*
JOSEPHINE DE BRISSAC	*Catherine Willmer*
PIXIE ('I'LL GET MY MAN') POTTER	*Jane Lapotaire*
THE BISHOP OF LAX	*Philip King*

The Play directed by Denis Carey

Designed by Catherine Browne

SYNOPSIS OF SCENES

The action of the play passes in the lounge-hall of the Vicarage, in the small village of Stebbington-Fawley

ACT I

9 a.m. on a bright spring Monday morning

ACT II

SCENE 1   10 a.m. the following Thursday
SCENE 2   The next morning

ACT III

One second later

Time—the present

iii

I'LL GET MY MAN

ACT I

SCENE—*The lounge-hall of the Vicarage in the small village of Stebbington-Fawley. 9 a.m. on a bright spring Monday.*

The room is somewhat old-fashioned; chintzy, but very comfortable and pleasant to look at. The main exit, to the front door, is down L. *A staircase leads off up* L *from up* C. L *of this is the door to the kitchen. Large french windows up* RC *lead to the garden. There is no fireplace, that, presumably, being in the 'fourth wall'. By the window, up* R, *is a large screen. There is a desk down* R *and a settee* LC. *A gate-legged table, covered with a large tablecloth, is set for breakfast and stands* C. RC *is an armchair.*

When the CURTAIN *rises, the* REVEREND ARTHUR HUMPHREY *is discovered seated at the table facing the audience. He is a mild little cleric of about forty-five. At the moment he cannot be seen as he has 'The Times' open in front of him. While reading the paper he sings quietly to himself from 'The Mikado'.*

HUMPHREY (*singing*) 'The flowers that bloom in the spring,
            Tra la,
      Have nothing to do with the case.'

(*The head and shoulders of* MRS CARTER *come furtively round the kitchen door. She is a talkative but good-looking 'help', aged between thirty-five and forty*)

            'I've got to take under my wing,
            Tra la,
            A most unattractive old thing,
            Tra, la . . .'

MRS CARTER (*interrupting the song; conspiratorially*) Sssssssss!

(HUMPHREY *lowers the paper. He is now seen to be wearing his clerical collar and bib over a white shirt, but no jacket. He looks towards Mrs Carter*)

HUMPHREY (*quite cheerfully*) Ah! Good morning, Mrs Carter! and what a lovely spring morning it is!

MRS CARTER (*still only head and shoulders showing*) 'Asn't come down yet, 'as she?

HUMPHREY. No, no. Not yet.

1

MRS CARTER (*with satisfaction*) Aaah! (*She comes into the room. In her hand she has a small plate with two sausages on it*) Then get these down you before she does! (*She puts the plate on the table in front of Humphrey*)

HUMPHREY (*beaming*) Sausages! Mrs Carter . . . !

MRS CARTER. Never mind 'Mrs Carter-in' '; get 'em down. (*She moves to a small table below the stairs and, almost automatically, picks up a large silver-framed photograph of a handsome young man. She gives it a big noisy kiss. To the photograph*) 'Mornin' my lovely! (*She replaces it*)

HUMPHREY (*whose attention is on the sausages; taking a bite*) They're delicious! (*He holds it in his hand*)

MRS CARTER (*moving to him*) That's what Carter said at breakfast, but he could only manage five. Them's left-overs.

HUMPHREY (*taking another bite*) Delicious!

MRS CARTER. I daren't 'ot 'em up. That sister of yours has a nose like an 'awk—she'd've been sure to smell 'em.

HUMPHREY. I shouldn't be eating them, you know. I feel very guilty.

MRS CARTER (*practically*) Right! Give 'em me back; my chickens'll be glad of 'em. (*She makes to take the plate away*)

HUMPHREY (*with a little yelp; putting his hands over the plate to protect it*) No! I—I don't feel as guilty as all that!

MRS CARTER (*with a sniff*) I should think not indeed! (*With another sniff*) Puttin' you on a diet—I never 'eard such tommy-rot!

HUMPHREY. Oh, but it's true what Harriette says. I am developing quite a—a tummy.

MRS CARTER. Well, what if you are! I mean—nobody's goin' to think you're pregnant.

HUMPHREY. Mrs Carter!

MRS CARTER. And you can still squeeze into the pulpit, can't you?

HUMPHREY. Good heavens, yes!

MRS CARTER. Then what you want to be dieting for?

HUMPHREY. My sister says I'm eating the wrong kinds of food; that is why I'm inclined to be—er—forgetful occasionally.

MRS CARTER. Course, you know what *you* want, really, don't you?

HUMPHREY (*holding up the sausage*) I'm very content at the moment!

MRS CARTER (*firmly*) A wife—that's what you want.

HUMPHREY. A wife? (*He gulps*)

MRS CARTER. Someone to love and cherish you.

HUMPHREY (*musing*) Yes—yes—very nice—love and cherish —and cook!

MRS CARTER. 'Aven't you never thought about it—gettin' married?

HUMPHREY. Oh, yes indeed! I've *thought* about it.

MRS CARTER. Well you ought to think a bit 'arder! And now's the time to do it—you *know*—spring—the matin' season . . .

HUMPHREY (*somewhat shocked*) Mrs Carter!

MRS CARTER (*firmly*) Now it's no use you gettin' all 'ot under the dog-collar. Parson though you may be, you know how many beans make five.

HUMPHREY (*sighing*) It has always been the wish of my life that *someday—someone*—but—at my age—who would . . . ?

MRS CARTER. You know what they say—Miss Right's always round the corner.

HUMPHREY (*horrified*) Miss *Wright?* Good heavens! I *know* she's round the corner—been there for years—but she's eighty if she's a day!

MRS CARTER (*exasperated*) I don't mean that Miss Wright. I mean—the *right* one.

HUMPHREY. Oh! Oh, yes, I see! Miss *Right!*

MRS CARTER (*moving to the table up* C *and dusting*) She wouldn't stand no nonsense from your sister, Miss Right wouldn't! Soon give 'er 'er marching orders.

HUMPHREY. But Harriette wouldn't hear of my getting married. She'd disapprove most strongly.

MRS CARTER. Not much use her disapprovin' once you'd done it.

HUMPHREY. Now, Mrs Carter, you must stop talking like this. Good heavens! You're putting ideas into my head!

MRS CARTER (*picking up the silver-framed photograph again*) I'll bet *he* wouldn't let his sister rule *him!*

HUMPHREY. Who? Oh, Peter! No, no, I don't suppose he would—but he hasn't got a sister.

MRS CARTER (*gazing at the photograph adoringly*) Oo! Isn't he 'eaven! And to think he's your nephew—your own flesh and blood, so to speak. Aren't you proud of him?

HUMPHREY. Oh, yes, indeed! Very proud.

MRS CARTER. I should just think you are. I mean—'im being on the telly every week! He's my pin-up boy—my 'eart-throb. I'm just mad about him. I can't help it! When he comes on the telly and I look at '*im*, then I look across at Carter, I think to myself 'My God!'

HUMPHREY (*reprovingly*) 'T! 't! 't!

MRS CARTER (*unheeding*) Did you watch *Venture Man* last night? (*Then to the photograph, giving it another noisy kiss*) Bless you! (*She replaces the photograph*)

HUMPHREY. Unfortunately, no. I wasn't able to. Most disappointing, but I had a Church Council Meeting. I tried to hurry it through, but . . . Ahem! (*He coughs, embarrassed*)

MRS CARTER. Peter was smashin'—best ever! And when he jumped into that ragin' sea, full of deadly sharks . . . !

HUMPHREY. Goodness gracious! Did he do that?

MRS CARTER. True as I'm standing 'ere! He isn't called 'Venture Man' for nothing!

HUMPHREY. I hope the raging sea was warm. He's always been inclined to be a bit chesty.

(MRS CARTER *rushes to the photograph, picks it up and talks to it*)

MRS CARTER. Oh, the poor lamb! And you'd nothing on but your trousers, 'ad you, my lovely, and I thought one minute *they* were comin' off!

(*A door slams upstairs*)

(*At once alarmed; putting the photograph down*) That's 'er door! Miss 'Umphrey's!

HUMPHREY (*placatingly*) There's nothing to be alarmed about, Mrs Carter.

MRS CARTER. Isn't there? You've still got some sausage left!

HUMPHREY (*at once panic-stricken*) Oh!

(HUMPHREY *pops the remainder of the sausage into his mouth and promptly chokes and splutters.* MRS CARTER *rushes and thumps him on the back*)

MRS CARTER (*alarmed; as she thumps*) Stop it! Give over! Be quiet, do you hear?

HUMPHREY (*spluttering*) I—I . . . (*He chokes and splutters again as another thump lands on his back*)

MRS CARTER (*accusingly*) You'll 'ave us both 'ung! (*Her eyes fall on the plate she brought in*) Oh my . . . ! (*She grabs the plate quickly and puts it under her pinafore*)

(HUMPHREY *is still spluttering and choking.* MRS CARTER *is still thumping as* HARRIETTE HUMPHREY *appears at the top of the stairs.* HARRIETTE *is a couple of years older than Humphrey, angular, staid and somewhat vinegary*)

HARRIETTE (*taking in the scene*) What on earth is going on? Arthur, what *is* the matter with you?

MRS CARTER (*promptly*) Asthma!

HARRIETTE. What?

MRS CARTER. Brought on by starvation—that's what!

HARRIETTE (*descending the stairs*) Don't talk nonsense. More likely apoplexy—brought on by over-eating.

MRS CARTER (*with derision*) After what he's had in this 'ouse in the last four days? I'll tell the birds and the bees!

HARRIETTE (*coldly*) Will you kindly bring the breakfast in now, Mrs Carter. (*She moves* L *of the table*)

MRS CARTER. *Breakfast?* I'd blush to give it to a skeleton for its elevenses . . . (*She begins to move towards the kitchen*)

HARRIETTE. And, Mrs Carter ...

MRS CARTER. Yes?

HARRIETTE (*picking up the butter dish from the table and handing it to her*) We shall *not* require the butter.

MRS CARTER (*as she moves quickly to the kitchen door*) Gawd in 'eaven!

(MRS CARTER *exits to the kitchen*)

HARRIETTE (*having glanced at Humphrey again; moving to open the french windows*) Arthur!

HUMPHREY. Yes, Harriette?

HARRIETTE. Your jacket! (*She starts doing breathing exercises*)

HUMPHREY. My ... (*He looks at himself*) I haven't got it on.

HARRIETTE. There's nothing wrong with my eyesight, Arthur! You *forgot* to put it on, I presume.

HUMPHREY (*limply*) I—I *intended* putting it on.

HARRIETTE (*shortly*) Intended! If there is any truth in the saying that the downward path is paved with good intentions, Arthur, *you* must be teetering on the very *brink* of hell!

HUMPHREY (*vaguely*) Talking about breakfast ...

HARRIETTE. We are *not* talking about breakfast.

HUMPHREY. Not? Oh well—I was thinking about it—it's the same thing, isn't it?

HARRIETTE. Really, Arthur, your absentmindedness these days ... quite alarming! You appear at table half naked ...

HUMPHREY. Harriette!

HARRIETTE. Look, the other morning, when you appeared without even your ...

HUMPHREY (*hurriedly*) Yes, dear, but that was one of my—er—bad days.

HARRIETTE. Your bad days are beginning to outnumber the good ones.

(MRS CARTER *enters from the kitchen carrying a tray on which are a small pot of coffee, two small glasses of barley water, a toast rack containing four 'Ryvita-type' biscuits, and a small bowl in which is what appears to be a bundle of straw*)

(*Moving* R *of the table*) Ah! Breakfast at last!

MRS CARTER (*as she approaches the table*) Well for *what* it is, and *such* as it is, here it is. (*She puts the things from the tray on to the table*)

HUMPHREY (*dolefully*) Thank you, Mrs Carter.

MRS CARTER. You're welcome to it, I'm sure. If I was to put a breakfast like that in front of Carter, he'd throw *it*—*and* me—straight through the kitchen window!

HARRIETTE (*picking up a small milk jug*) This isn't cream, is it?

MRS CARTER (*derisively*) Cream? It's that blue I thought it was watered ink.

HARRIETTE (*coldly*) It will do very nicely, thank you.
MRS CARTER (*as she goes*) Not for Carter it wouldn't!

(MRS CARTER *exits to the kitchen*)

HARRIETTE (*sitting* R *of the table*) Mrs Carter is getting quite beyond herself. Drink your barley water.
HUMPHREY (*sipping his barley water and wincing*) She's a good worker, Harriette.
HARRIETTE. If she wasn't, she'd have been sent packing long ago. (*She pours coffee*)
HUMPHREY. And a wonderful cook! (*With a sigh*) Those heavenly breakfasts I—I *used* to have! Those delicious kidneys on Mondays—and that lovely bacon and crispy golden-brown fried bread on Tuesdays! And those luscious mushrooms on toast, with warmed-up potato on Wednesdays—and those . . .
HARRIETTE (*sharply*) Arthur, get on with your 'Shreddi-wex'!
HUMPHREY (*blinking*) My shreddi what?
HARRIETTE (*pointing to the small bowl*) That!
HUMPHREY. It sounds like furniture polish! (*He sticks a fork into the 'Shreddi-wex' and lifts it up*) And it looks like a forsaken bird's nest!
HARRIETTE. Never mind what it looks like. It's good for you—very slimming. Pass me the *Daily Mail*.

(HUMPHREY *passes her a folded copy of the 'Daily Mail'. He then stabs dejectedly at his 'Shreddi-wex' with a fork*)

(*As she unfolds the paper*) Have you any appointments this morning?
HUMPHREY (*still stabbing, almost fascinated*) No, no, I don't think so.
HARRIETTE. You'd better consult your diary to make sure; your mind in the disorderly state it is. I have a meeting at ten o'clock at the Institute.
HUMPHREY (*sticking his fork into his 'Shreddi-wex'*) Oh?
HARRIETTE. Our new campaign.
HUMPHREY (*vaguely*) 'Votes for Women?' (*He picks up the sugar caster*)
HARRIETTE (*acidly*) 'Freedom from Hunger.' (*She takes the caster and puts it down*)

(HUMPHREY *gives a loud groan*)

(*Glancing at the front page of the paper*) We're sending several parcels off this morning—to Bulawayo (*Opening the paper*)
HUMPHREY (*wretchedly; holding out the 'Shreddi-wex' on his fork*) You wouldn't care to send . . . ? (*Then, reflectively*) No, perhaps not! In any case, it looks as if it *came* from there!
HARRIETTE (*suddenly—as she reads something*) Oh no!
HUMPHREY. Well, *near* there.

HARRIETTE (*still gaping at the paper*) I don't believe it!

HUMPHREY (*still looking at his 'Shreddi-wex'*) Well, it was never made in England!

HARRIETTE. Arthur! Have you seen this in the paper about Peter?

HUMPHREY (*releasing the 'Shreddi-wex' from the fork and back into the bowl*) Peter? Peter?

HARRIETTE (*acidly*) Our *nephew* Peter!

HUMPHREY (*still concentrating on the 'Shreddi-wex'*) Oh, *Peter!* No, my dear. What's happened? Has he landed an even bigger television contract?

HARRIETTE (*with a snort*) It looks as if he's landed himself in a whole lot of trouble.

HUMPHREY (*gaping at the 'Shreddi-wex'*) Goodness gracious! Harriette! This—this 'Shreddi-thing'—it *moved!* I'm sure it did! I saw it! It—sort of—jumped!

HARRIETTE. Will you stop talking nonsense and listen to this!

HUMPHREY. But, Harriette ... ! (*He moves the bowl away from him, puts a plate over it, and the milk jug on top of the plate*)

HARRIETTE (*irritably*) Are you listening, Arthur?

HUMPHREY. It did move, Harriette! It sort of—hopped! But don't worry. I've battened it down now. It can't get out. (*Blandly*) What were you saying, my dear?

HARRIETTE (*exasperated*) Really! I am trying to tell you about Peter.

HUMPHREY. *What* about him?

HARRIETTE. He's going to get married!

HUMPHREY (*sighing*) Lucky Peter!

HARRIETTE. To one of those dreadful Pop-Singer creatures.

HUMPHREY. A Beatle?

HARRIETTE. Listen to this! (*Reading*) The heading is 'Has he been caught at last?' Then it goes on: 'Our photograph shows Peter (Venture Man) Graham, television's highest-paid star and —incidentally—most eligible bachelor; and the heart-throb of millions of women, dining with this month's "Top-of-the-Pops" girl, Pixie (I'll Get My Man) Potter, in a quiet Soho restaurant last Saturday night. Toying prettily with her Crepe Suzette, Pixie said, "I have adored Peter from the first moment I saw him in *Venture Man!*" Can it be that Pixie, whose latest record "I'll Get My Man" is Number One in the Hit Parade, has actually—*got her man?* My bet is—she has!' (*Lowering the paper*) Disgusting!

(MRS CARTER *dashes in from the kitchen waving a 'Daily Mirror' in her hand*)

MRS CARTER (*as she enters*) Have you seen it?

HARRIETTE (*frigidly*) Mrs Carter, really! You mustn't come bursting into the room like that!

MRS CARTER (*moving between Harriette and Humphrey*) I know I mustn't, but I've just seen it in the paper about *him*. Peter!

HARRIETTE. If you mean our nephew . . .

MRS CARTER (*with a wail*) He's going to get married! (*Thrusting the paper forward*) Oo! (*With a break in her voice*) I can't bear to think of it! That big, gorgeous 'ulk of 'usky 'eart-throb——

HARRIETTE. Mrs Carter!

MRS CARTER. —married to that—that trollop!

HARRIETTE. Mrs Carter, I must ask you . . .

MRS CARTER (*holding the paper practically under Harriette's nose*) Well, have you *seen* her? (*Then putting the paper under Humphrey's nose*) And I'll swear she hasn't had a comb through her hair for months! And to think of her snaffling that gorgeous 'ulk of 'usky! (*With a wail*) It won't bear thinking about! He could've 'ad any woman in the country he'd wanted. (*Wildly*) He could've 'ad me!

HARRIETTE. *Mrs Carter!*

MRS CARTER. I'd've left Carter for him any day! But no! He has to go and let himself be tricked into marrying that little 'orror! And what's she got to offer him? Nothing—except a bust!

HARRIETTE (*fuming*) Mrs Carter, I must ask you . . .

MRS CARTER (*to Humphrey; unheeding*) You've got to stop him, sir!

HUMPHREY (*blinking*) I? But . . .

MRS CARTER. You've *got* to—for the sake of all the women in England.

HARRIETTE. Mrs Carter, will you please pull yourself together!

MRS CARTER. No, I won't! Not till the Vicar's promised! He'll listen to you, sir; you're his uncle.

HARRIETTE (*frigidly*) I am also his aunt.

MRS CARTER. I *know*—poor lad!

HARRIETTE. Oh!

HUMPHREY (*quickly*) I—I—I'll try to speak to him on the phone, Mrs Carter. I'll tell him what you say.

MRS CARTER. Bless you, sir! Bless you! Bless you! (*She kisses his head*) Stop 'im from doing this terrible thing and there isn't an angel in 'eaven that won't sing your praises!

HUMPHREY (*puzzled*) But—surely—they don't watch *Venture Man* up there?

HARRIETTE (*shocked*) Arthur! (*To Mrs Carter*) And now, Mrs Carter, if you will kindly return to the kitchen . . . !

MRS CARTER (*distrait*) I will. (*Moving up* L) But what good I'll be when I get there . . . And 'eaven 'elp any crockery that gets in my way this morning!

(MRS CARTER *exits to the kitchen*)

HARRIETTE (*rising and moving* LC) It's no use, Arthur. We shall have to get rid of that woman. She's becoming utterly impossible.

HUMPHREY. But where would we find anyone who can cook like Mrs Carter?

HARRIETTE. Really! Can't you think of anything except your stomach? I *have* cooked for us in the past, don't forget.

HUMPHREY (*wincing*) I shall *never* forget!

HARRIETTE. I have more important things to deal with than cooking. Don't forget I practically run this parish for you.

HUMPHREY (*with a sigh*) You know, it's a great pity you never married, Harriette. You would have made some parson a wonderful wife.

HARRIETTE (*moving down* L; *snorting*) I've had to look after you, haven't I? I've never been able to give a thought to marriage. Have you finished your breakfast?

HUMPHREY. No, dear. It's finished me!

(MRS CARTER *comes in with a tray from the kitchen*)

HARRIETTE. What is it, Mrs Carter?

MRS CARTER. Thought you might like to know Mrs Barrington-Locke's just turned into the drive.

HARRIETTE (*with a wail*) Oh no!

MRS CARTER. Oh *yes*.

HARRIETTE. Winifred! (*Moving* R) Really I can *not* cope with her eccentricity at this hour of the morning.

MRS CARTER. I wouldn't mind bein' a bit round the bend with her money!

HARRIETTE. Arthur, she isn't coming to see you, is she?

HUMPHREY. Goodness gracious, I hope not! Frightens the life out of me!

HARRIETTE. Then if you don't want to see her you'd better go upstairs out of the way. And, Arthur, do please finish dressing.

HUMPHREY. Yes, dear (*He folds his napkin*)

MRS CARTER. Shall I bring some more coffee in?

HARRIETTE. No, no! Do that and she'll be here till lunchtime. (*She moves to the table and picks up the coffee-pot*) What you can do is take this out! (*She goes towards Mrs Carter with the coffee-pot*)

(HUMPHREY, *having folded his napkin, rises and moves away from the table to* R. *He is now seen to be without his trousers*)

MRS CARTER. I could tell her you're not at . . . (*She suddenly gives a scream—her eyes on Humphrey*) Oh, sir!

HARRIETTE (*turning*) What . . . ? *Arthur!*

HUMPHREY (*vaguely*) What, Harriette?

HARRIETTE. *You've done it again!*
HUMPHREY. What?
HARRIETTE (*pointing; frantically*) Your . . . !

(MRS CARTER *is not shocked, but thoroughly amused*)

HUMPHREY (*after looking down; in horror*) Oh!

(*A hearty female voice is heard off down* L. *It belongs to* MRS BARRINGTON-LOCKE)

MRS BARRINGTON-LOCKE (*off*) Anyone at home? Can I come in?

(HARRIETTE *and* HUMPHREY *give yelps of alarm*)

HARRIETTE (*to Humphrey; frantically*) Go! Go!

(HUMPHREY *makes hastily towards the window*)

(*More frantically*) Not into the garden! The whole village will . . .
MRS BARRINGTON-LOCKE (*nearer*) You in here?

(HUMPHREY *now makes as if to dash for the stairs, but* HARRIETTE *stops him and pushes him back*)
HARRIETTE. There isn't time! Quickly—behind there!
HUMPHREY. Where?

(HARRIETTE *pushes him behind the screen. He is only just out of sight when* MRS BARRINGTON-LOCKE *enters down* L.
MRS BARRINGTON-LOCKE *is a fairly large, forthright, 'don't-give-me-any-nonsense' type of woman of forty*)

MRS BARRINGTON-LOCKE (*halting in the archway*) Ah, there you are? You all deaf? I've been bawling my lungs out! 'Morning, good morning, good morning!
HUMPHREY (*from behind the screen; tremulously*) Good morning!

(HARRIETTE *gives a little start and backs to the screen*)

MRS BARRINGTON-LOCKE (*having heard Humphrey*) What . . .? Who said . . . ?

(MRS CARTER *comes quickly to the rescue*)

MRS CARTER (*to Harriette*) Shall I clear'm? (*She proceeds to put things from the table on to a tray*)

(MRS BARRINGTON-LOCKE *looks distinctly puzzled*)

MRS BARRINGTON-LOCKE. I . . . I thought I heard a man's voice.
HARRIETTE (*with a harassed smile*) Did you?
MRS BARRINGTON-LOCKE. D'y'mean did I *think* I did, or did I hear it? I'm damn' sure I did!
HARRIETTE (*embarrassed by the 'damn'*) Er—Winifred—(*she indicates Mrs Carter*)—language!

Mrs Carter (*seeing this*) Oh, you don't have to worry about me. You should hear Carter when he lets off steam!

Mrs Barrington-Locke (*interested*) Really?

Mrs Carter. Cor'! What a performance!

Mrs Barrington-Locke (*moving to the settee*) You'd better send him up to the Grange sometime.

Harriette (*almost bleating*) Winifred!

Mrs Barrington-Locke (*unheeding, grinning*) Got quite a vocabulary, eh?

Mrs Carter. He can let rip for five minutes without stoppin', and never use the same word twice.

Harriette (*trying to be firm*) Mrs Carter, will you . . .

Mrs Carter (*equally firmly*) No, I will not! If you want to hear 'em, you'll hear 'em from Carter—not from me!

Harriette. Thank you, Mrs Carter, you may go. (*She waves towards the kitchen*)

(Mrs Barrington-Locke *sits on the settee*)

Mrs Carter (*having seen that Mrs Barrington-Locke's back is towards them; hoarsely*) But what about . . . ? (*She waves frantically towards the screen*)

(Harriette *waves her hands to stop Mrs Carter waving.* Mrs Barrington-Locke *turns, and, unseen by the others, watches them*)

Shall I go— (*she gestures 'upstairs'*) and get his—— (*She is gesturing 'trousers', when she realizes Mrs Barrington-Locke is watching her. With a false laugh, she picks up the tray and dashes towards the kitchen, speaking as she goes*) Lovely wash-day, Mrs Barrington-Locke!

(Mrs Carter *exits to the kitchen*)

Mrs Barrington-Locke (*after watching her go*) And what was all that about?

(Harriette *folds the table-cloth, then folds the gate-legged table and puts it, with the cloth on it, down* l)

Harriette. All what?

Mrs Barrington-Locke. All that (*demonstrating*) 'tic-tacking, between you and Mrs Carter.

Harriette (*uneasily*) Oh, nothing. (*She moves to the screen*) We were just—er . . . You're—you're out and about very early, aren't you?

Mrs Barrington-Locke (*searching in her handbag*) Well, when you're a widow, what is there to stop in bed for?

(*From behind the screen comes a loud gasp, followed by a short burst of embarrassed coughing.* Mrs Barrington-Locke *looks up and round, sharply.* HARRIETTE *puts her hand to her chest, as if she had just been coughing)*

(Seeing this; puzzled) That's a hell of a bark you've got, Harriette!

HARRIETTE *(flustered)* Winifred . . . really . . .

MRS BARRINGTON-LOCKE. Look, Harriette, don't stand there dithering. Come and sit down. I want a little advice.

HARRIETTE. Oh, but . . .

MRS BARRINGTON-LOCKE *(continuing, unheeding)* You know; woman to woman.

(Again the embarrassed cough from behind the screen. Again, HARRIETTE *puts her hand to her chest)*

(Again puzzled) Good lord, Harriette! That cough of yours! *(Looking away)* Like a sex-starved walrus calling its mate!

(Again the cough—a squeaky one this time—from behind the screen. Again MRS BARRINGTON-LOCKE *spins round)*

HARRIETTE *(desperately)* Couldn't we talk better in the garden?

MRS BARRINGTON-LOCKE *(firmly)* No. We couldn't. *(She puts on horn-rimmed glasses—from her bag)*

HARRIETTE *(moving towards* C*)* But it's quite warm. We could sit out on the lawn. *(She puts one chair from the* C *table below the stairs, then the other under the small table up* C*)*

MRS BARRINGTON-LOCKE. I am sitting on *no* lawn! If *you* don't mind 'em, I do! *(She now produces a previously opened envelope)*

HARRIETTE. Mind what?

MRS BARRINGTON-LOCKE. Ants in my pants.

(There is a spluttering noise from HUMPHREY *behind the screen.* HARRIETTE *backs towards the screen)*

(Looking up, straight ahead, then removing her glasses and looking slowly round at Harriette) You need an Alka Seltzer, don't you?

HARRIETTE *(gaping)* What?

MRS BARRINGTON-LOCKE. That *was* your stomach rumbling, wasn't it?

HARRIETTE *(shocked)* Pardon?

MRS BARRINGTON-LOCKE. Granted. *(Replacing her glasses)* Well now—to business! Harriette, I've had a proposal. *(Holding up the envelope)*

HARRIETTE *(still very distrait)* What to do? *(She moves* RC*)*

MRS BARRINGTON-LOCKE *(blinking at Harriette over her glasses)* What to do? To get *married*, of course, you nit!

HARRIETTE. Married? *You?*

MRS BARRINGTON-LOCKE. There's no need to sound so damned

incredulous. After all, why shouldn't I marry again? I've still got lots of the old Adam—or Eve—or whatever you like to call it, in me.

HARRIETTE (*feebly*) Winifred, please . . . !

MRS BARRINGTON-LOCKE (*unheeding*) And I'm healthy! Fit as a fiddle! Matter of fact, I went to see old Doc' Foster for a check-up only the other day. And what a caper *that* was! Had me stretched out on his table stark . . .

HARRIETTE (*looking towards the screen; wildly*) Winifred!

(HUMPHREY'S *head appears over the screen, listening*)

MRS BARRINGTON-LOCKE (*overlapping*) Prodded me here, prodded me there, put me through a sort of 'knees up Mother Brown', pummelled me all over, and, after all that, gave me a heck of slap on the rump and said, 'Winnie, my girl, you're good for another fifty years!' (*With pride*) So—what do you think of *that*?

HUMPHREY. Amazing! (*He bobs quickly out of sight*)

(MRS BARRINGTON-LOCKE *quickly removes her glasses and looks round, completely puzzled*)

MRS BARRINGTON-LOCKE (*having looked around*) Did you hear that?

HARRIETTE (*moving up by the screen again*) What?

MRS BARRINGTON-LOCKE (*baffled, poking her finger in her ear*) P'raps I'm not as fit as I thought I was. I'm beginning to hear things. What was I talking about? Ah, yes! I tell you again—I've had a proposal of marriage.

HARRIETTE (*still distrait*) And . . . er . . . are you going to accept?

MRS BARRINGTON-LOCKE. What? Marry old George Patterson? Last time I saw him he was propped up on two sticks. Expect he's on three by now! (*Chuckling*) Marry old George!

HARRIETTE (*with a glance towards the screen*) Well, if you're not going to marry the man . . .

MRS BARRINGTON-LOCKE. What would be the point? What use would *he* be? No! I'm not going to marry *George*, but—him proposing to me—it's put ideas into my head! I thought it over, after I got his letter this morning—while I was ploughing through the old bacon and egg, and I thought to myself, Winnie, old girl, why shouldn't you get married again? Not to George, of course, but—dammit, a fine strapping healthy chunk of womanhood like you—it's your *duty*!

HARRIETTE (*vaguely*) Duty to whom?

MRS BARRINGTON-LOCKE (*flummoxed*) *I* dunno! The country, I suppose! It can do with a few more Young Conservatives. You don't happen to know of any likely candidate for the Marriage Stakes, do you, Harriette?

HARRIETTE (*blinking*) I . . . (*She sits in the armchair* RC) How should I know?

MRS BARRINGTON-LOCKE. Well, dammit, you get around more than I do—all these committees you're on, and charities you collect for . . .

HARRIETTE (*coldly*) I collect money—not eligible men!

MRS BARRINGTON-LOCKE (*with a grin*) What would *you* do with an eligible man? You wouldn't know where to start on him!

HARRIETTE. Winifred!

MRS BARRINGTON-LOCKE (*reflectively*) I wonder what's become of Wally?

HARRIETTE. Wally?

(HUMPHREY's *head appears again*)

MRS BARRINGTON-LOCKE (*nodding; grinning*) Thinkin' back a bit now, old girl—back to my twenties! A young blood I used to know at Cambridge. He was at Kings—I was at Boots—Cosmetiques! Wonder if *he's* still standing on his own two legs! Damn' good legs they were too! (*Laughing to herself*) Now—if Wally were around—and active—*and* unattached . . . (*She growls sexily*)

(HUMPHREY *growls also, then bobs down.* MRS BARRINGTON-LOCKE *looks up quickly, then towards Harriette*)

(*Grinning*) Givin' you ideas, old girl?

HARRIETTE. Winifred!

MRS BARRINGTON-LOCKE (*rising*) Anyway, keep your eyes open, and if you do come across something that *can* stand on its own two legs, and you think might be suitable . . . Of course, come to think of it, I could always advertise . . .

HARRIETTE (*rising; shocked*) Advertise—for a—a husband?

MRS BARRINGTON-LOCKE. Why not? Been done before, y'know.

HARRIETTE. Winifred!

MRS BARRINGTON-LOCKE. 'Lonely widow wishes to meet . . .'

HARRIETTE. Oh really! You go too far.

MRS BARRINGTON-LOCKE. I haven't started yet! Haven't you ever heard that it pays to advertise? (*Consulting her watch*) Hey! I must be off! And I know you can't wait to get rid of me. (*She picks up her bag*)

HARRIETTE (*almost too eagerly*) I'll see you to the door.

MRS BARRINGTON-LOCKE (*moving* L) By the way, where's the Vicar?

HARRIETTE (*following; nervously*) Arthur?

MRS BARRINGTON-LOCKE. Isn't he around?

HARRIETTE. Oh yes, he's—around.

MRS BARRINGTON-LOCKE (*chuckling*) Waiting for me to go, eh? Dunno why, but I seem to scare the pants off him!

HARRIETTE. He hasn't got them . . . (*She pulls up quickly*)

MRS BARRINGTON-LOCKE (*still chuckling*) Well, you can tell him he might have a wedding on his hands very shortly. Oh, and by the way, Harriette, if you *do* come across a man you think might be suitable, make sure he's in good working order!

(MRS BARRINGTON-LOCKE *departs down* L)

HARRIETTE (*bleating, with hand to head*) Winifred . . . !

(HARRIETTE *exits down* L.

After a moment HUMPHREY'S *head comes cautiously round the screen. Seeing the room is empty he emerges from behind the screen. He is obviously very excited and delighted. He stands still for a moment, then unable to control his excitement begins to sing and clap his hands as he does a little dance round the room*)

HUMPHREY (*singing; from 'The Mikado'*)
          'For he's going to marry Yum-Yum
          Yum-Yum!
          Your anger pray bury,
          For all will be merry,
          I think you had better succumb—
          Cumb-cumb.'

(*He stops dancing for a moment, then carried away, begins again more vigorously*)
          'For he's going to marry Yum-Yum
          Yum-Yum . . .'

(MRS CARTER *enters from the kitchen. She brings a Hoover with her*)

MRS CARTER (*seeing him dancing; leaving the Hoover and rushing to him*) Vicar!

HUMPHREY (*seizing Mrs Carter and whirling her round*)
          'Your anger pray bury,
          For all will be merry,
          I think you had better succumb—
          Cumb-cumb.'

MRS CARTER (*breathlessly*) Sir—what is it? What's happened? Have you gone stark-staring . . .

HUMPHREY (*happily*) No, no, Mrs Carter! I've got an idea! A wonderful idea!

MRS CARTER. I've got one too. 'Adn't you better get your trousers on before Miss 'Umphrey . . .

HUMPHREY. I'm not thinking about my trousers.

MRS CARTER. I know you aren't, but *she* will!

HUMPHREY (*suddenly*) It pays to advertise, Mrs Carter!

MRS CARTER (*gaping at him*) What?

HUMPHREY (*wildly*) Advertise! And if Harriette continues with this diet . . .

MRS CARTER. I don't know what you're . . .

HUMPHREY (*seizing her by the hands again, and dancing her round as he sings*)
> 'Your anger pray bury,
> For all will be merry,
> I think you had better succumb—
> Cumb-cumb.'

(*During the last line,* HARRIETTE *enters down* L. *She stops in the archway, horrified*)

HARRIETTE. *Arthur!*

HUMPHREY (*at once embarrassed and deflated*) Oh—er—Harriette!

HARRIETTE. Have you taken leave of your senses altogether?

HUMPHREY. I—I . . .

HARRIETTE (*at bursting point*) Arthur, if you don't go upstairs at once and get some trousers on . . . !

MRS CARTER. You don't 'ave to worry about that, not as far as I'm concerned. More often than not Carter roams around the house in far less than his trousers.

HARRIETTE. Mrs Carter, I . . .

MRS CARTER (*placidly*) I'm only telling you.

(*The telephone on the desk rings*)

HUMPHREY ⎫
HARRIETTE ⎭ (*together*) I'll answer it!

(*They both move quickly to the phone.* HUMPHREY *gets there first*)

HARRIETTE. Arthur, you can't! Not without your . . .

HUMPHREY (*into the phone*) The Vicarage, Stebbington-Fawley.

(HUMPHREY *sits in the swivel desk-chair*)

HARRIETTE (*rushing and grabbing the tablecloth and bringing it quickly to Humphrey; holding it out*) Put this round you!

HUMPHREY (*vaguely, as he listens to the phone, taking the cloth and putting it under him*) Oh, thank you, Harriette. It *is* rather cold!

HARRIETTE (*furiously*) Oh!

HUMPHREY (*into the phone*) The Vicarage, Stebbington-Fawley. The Vicar speaking . . . Oh! Good morning, Lady McAlpine! (*Lowering the phone; to Harriette*) Harriette, it's Lady McAlpine.

HARRIETTE (*under her breath*) Lady Chatterbox!

HUMPHREY (*into the phone*) How are you, Lady Chatterley?

HARRIETTE (*almost a shriek*) Arthur!

HUMPHREY (*into the phone*) Lady McAlpine?

(MRS CARTER *sniggers, and plugs in the Hoover up* C)

HARRIETTE. 'T! 't! 't!

HUMPHREY (*into the phone*) Yes, you *are*; *quite* an early bird! (*Innocently*) But of course, *you're* a widow too——

(HARRIETTE *spins round*)

—with nothing to stop in bed for.

HARRIETTE (*with a shriek*) Arthur! (*She collapses into the armchair*)

HUMPHREY (*into the phone*) Er—what did you say? . . . 'Naughty, naughty'? (*Lowering the phone; rather pleased*) Lady McAlpine says I'm naughty, Harriette!

HARRIETTE (*frantically*) Will you get rid of her before you . . .

HUMPHREY. Yes, dear (*Into the phone*) Harriette says I'm to get rid of . . .

HARRIETTE (*leaping up*) No! No!

HUMPHREY (*after a quick look towards Harriette; into the phone*) Oh, I misunderstood her, apparently. I'm not to get rid of . . .

HARRIETTE (*waving a hand to stop him*) Yes, yes!

HUMPHREY (*swivelling round to the front, looking at Harriette, but unconsciously speaking into the phone*) Darling, do make up your mind! (*Then with a little yelp*) No, no! Not you, Lady McAlpine! I was talking to my sister . . . (*Unconsciously crossing his legs*) What was that? . . . You wish you could see me?

HARRIETTE (*feebly*) Arthur . . . ! (*She collapses into the chair*)

(MRS CARTER *almost leans on the Hoover handle, listening to all that goes on*)

MRS CARTER (*to Harriette; hoarsely*) It'd stop 'er chatter if she could!

HUMPHREY (*into the phone*) Well, why shouldn't you, Lady McAlpine? Come round right away! . . . No time like the present.

(HARRIETTE *whimpers.* MRS CARTER *giggles.* HUMPHREY *looks round at Harriette*)

(*into the phone*) You *can't* come round?

HARRIETTE (*glaring at him; fervently*) You should thank heaven for that!

HUMPHREY (*into the phone; his eyes on Harriette*) I thank heaven for . . .

HARRIETTE. *Arthur!*

HUMPHREY (*into the phone*) . . . H'm? . . . Peter? . . . Peter . . . Oh, yes, 'Venture Man'—our nephew . . . Oh, yes we saw it in the paper—at least Harriette did—she read it out to me . . . What's that? . . . You're heart-broken? . . . Oh, I am sorry, Lady

McALPINE. H'm? . . . You'd have married him yourself? (*To Harriette*) She'd have married him herself!

MRS CARTER (*indignantly and scornfully*) What, 'er? Tell 'er she's old enough to be his grandmother!

HUMPHREY (*into the phone*) You're old enough to be . . .

HARRIETTE (*beating her fists on the sides of the chair*) Oooh!

HUMPHREY (*into the phone*) What was that? . . . 'Stop Peter from . . .' . . . Oh, but I doubt whether he'd listen to *me* . . . Harriette? No, I'm *sure* he wouldn't listen to—— (*He coughs embarrassedly and looks round at Harriette*)

HARRIETTE (*fuming*) Ooooh!

HUMPHREY. . . . Well, Lady McAlpine, I will; I'll phone him immediately—(*speaking quite innocently*) and tell him exactly what you've told me to say to him, and I'm sure he'll tell me exactly what to say to you . . . Good-bye Lady McAlpine. Good-bye! (*He puts the receiver down*) Goodness gracious, how that woman talks! (*He picks up a small book from the desk*)

HARRIETTE (*springing to her feet and moving to the desk; fuming*) Arthur! I don't need to tell you I am a patient woman . . .

HUMPHREY (*preoccupied with his book*) Of course you don't.

HARRIETTE (*snatching the book from him*) You will go upstairs at once!

HUMPHREY. Oh, but—Peter . . .

HARRIETTE (*slamming the book down on the desk*) At once!

HUMPHREY (*rising; easily*) Very well, Harriette, if you say so. Come to think of it, I *am* feeling rather tired. (*Giving Harriette a kiss on the brow*) Good night, Harriette. (*Moving to the stairs*) I'm always glad when Sunday is over. (*He mounts the stairs*)

HARRIETTE (*almost barking*) Arthur!

HUMPHREY (*turning at the top of the stairs*) Yes, Harriette?

HARRIETTE (*trying to control herself*) It is *not* Sunday—it's Monday.

MRS CARTER (*laconically*) Wash-day.

HARRIETTE. And you are not going upstairs to bed; you are going to put on your . . .

HUMPHREY. Oh, yes, of course! I remember now. I'm sorry, Harriette. Very stupid of me. But Lady McAlpine . . .

HARRIETTE. *Will you listen to me?* (*Then almost as if to a child*) I have to go out . . .

HUMPHREY (*vaguely*) Splendid!

HARRIETTE (*after gulping*) I shall be going down to the Institute shortly.

HUMPHREY (*almost pained*) I know, my dear. You told me so; don't you remember?

(HARRIETTE *whimpers*)

You're sending some parcels off to—where is it now?

HARRIETTE (*almost pleased*) You see! You *can* remember when you make the effort! We're sending parcels of clothing to Bulawayo.

HUMPHREY. *That's* right! And you want my trousers.

(HUMPHREY *exits along the landing.* HARRIETTE *gives a wild cry and collapses into the chair* RC. MRS CARTER *moves near to Harriette and starts the Hoover.* HARRIETTE *gives another cry, and leaps to her feet*)

HARRIETTE (*loudly*) Stop that thing!

MRS CARTER (*hand to ear*) Pardon?

HARRIETTE (*louder*) I said . . . ! (*She rushes at the Hoover and switches it off*)

MRS CARTER (*puzzled*) You've stopped it!

HARRIETTE. My head's spinning enough, without . . .! What is the time? (*Consulting her watch*) I must go. (*Hand to head*) Now—that bundle of clothes I got ready—what did I do with it?

MRS CARTER. You mean that one by the front door?

HARRIETTE. Oh yes, of course! I put it there last night. You see—coping with my brother—it's getting me into the same state as he's in! (*As she crosses to the archway* L) I'll get it.

(HARRIETTE *exits down* L, *and returns almost immediately with a large bundle of drab-looking garments*)

MRS CARTER (*as* HARRIETTE *goes out; to herself*) Cor', and I was going to put 'em in the dustbin.

HARRIETTE (*just catching the word 'dustbin'*) What did you say?

MRS CARTER. Nothing.

(HARRIETTE *puts the bundle on the chair* RC *and begins to check it*)

(*Watching*) They're old clothes of *yours*, aren't they'm?

HARRIETTE (*sorting clothes*) They are. They're going to Bulawayo—though, my mind in the state it is, I'm just as likely to send them to Pakistan.

MRS CARTER. I shouldn't worry. If Pakistan gets 'em I'm sure Bulawayo'll be very grateful.

HARRIETTE *is about to speak sharply, but* MRS CARTER *cuts in*)

What about lunch'm?

HARRIETTE (*checking again*) *What* about it?

MRS CARTER. Well *what* about it?

HARRIETTE. What?

MRS CARTER. Well, what are you having?

HARRIETTE. There's a little cold meat left over from yesterday.

MRS CARTER. There is—a little. Will you have that?

HARRIETTE. Yes.

MRS CARTER. And what'll the Vicar have?

HARRIETTE. He'll have it too.

MRS CARTER (*outraged*) But it's only the size of an Oxo cube *now*—so when you cut it in half . . . !

HARRIETTE (*sharply*) There's lettuce in the garden—and radishes.

MRS CARTER. Yes'm! (*Slight pause*) And how many shall I give him?

HARRIETTE. What?

MRS CARTER. Radishes.

HARRIETTE. Mrs Carter, are you being facetious?

MRS CARTER. I don't know what that means, but I expect I am.

HARRIETTE. You can take my word for it—you *are*. You can also take a week's notice!

MRS CARTER. It's took! (*Moving to the kitchen door*) Where's me 'at?

HARRIETTE. I said a *week's* notice. You can't leave immediately.

MRS CARTER. What'you bet me?

HARRIETTE. Oooh!

(MRS CARTER *goes out to the kitchen*)

Objectionable creature! (*Muttering*) Let her go! (*She looks at her watch*) T! t! t! (*She crosses to the staircase and calls up it*) *Arthur!*

(HARRIETTE *then stalks off down* L, *and returns almost at once, wearing a large and completely shapeless hat. She crosses to the bundle, picks it up, then goes to the staircase again and calls louder and more impatiently*)

Arthur!

HUMPHREY (*off*) Were you calling, Harriette?

HARRIETTE. I was. Will you come down please!

HUMPHREY (*off*) Oh, but . . .

HARRIETTE (*louder*) At once! I want to make sure you're . . .

(HUMPHREY *appears on top of the stairs. He is now wearing a pair of baggy and rather short grey flannels and a shapeless sports jacket*)

(*Seeing this*) Oh, you are!

HUMPHREY. Of course I am—what?

HARRIETTE (*controlling herself*) I'm going now, Arthur.

HUMPHREY. Going? Oh yes, of course—the parcels—to Bulawayo.

HARRIETTE. Mrs Carter is going too.

HUMPHREY. To Bulawayo?

HARRIETTE (*after gulping*) Mrs Carter is leaving us.
HUMPHREY (*horrified*) Leaving! You don't mean . . . ?
HARRIETTE. I've dismissed her, Arthur. She's leaving *now*.
HUMPHREY. Oh no! Harriette! You can't . . . !
HARRIETTE. I have no time to stay arguing with you, Arthur.
In any case my mind is made up! (*Moving towards the french
windows*) Now—will you be going into the village this morning?
HUMPHREY. I—I—I . . .
HARRIETTE. Well, if you *do*, see that you lock the place up
first. There are some very odd-looking people around these days.
HUMPHREY (*looking at her, and the hat*) Yes, dear—*very* odd!

(HARRIETTE *departs through the french windows with the
bundle*)

(*Bewildered*) Mrs Carter—going . . . !

(MRS CARTER *comes through the kitchen door. She is wearing a hat*)

MRS CARTER. So you've 'eard, 'ave you?
HUMPHREY (*wretchedly*) Yes. (*He moves* RC)
MRS CARTER I *know*; I 'eard you 'earing! (*She jerks her head
towards the kitchen door*)
HUMPHREY. Mrs Carter—what can I say?
MRS CARTER (*sniffing a little*) There's nothing to say except
'good-bye' is there? (*She turns her head, and sees the photo-
graph*) Oh, and . . . ! (*Rushing to it and picking it up; snivelling*)
Good-bye, my lovely! (*She gives the photograph a big kiss*)
You're goin' to miss me, aren't you? And I'm goin' to miss you
. . . (*More snivelling*) I am—I am! Never mind! (*Beginning to
sing quietly in a quavering voice*)

'We'll meet again,
Dunno where, dunno when,
But I know we'll meet again
Some sunny day.'

(*She dissolves into tears and replaces the photograph*)

HUMPHREY. Mrs Carter. (*He is near to tears also*) I shall miss
you too—those luscious breakfasts you used to . . .
MRS CARTER (*suddenly pulling herself together*) She's gone
out, 'asn't she?
HUMPHREY. Er—Harriette? Yes.
MRS CARTER. Then do you know what I'm goin' to do before
I go?
HUMPHREY. No?
MRS CARTER. I'm goin' to cook you the best breakfast you're
likely to 'ave this side of the grave!
HUMPHREY (*delighted*) Mrs Carter!

MRS CARTER (*moving to the kitchen*) Bacon, eggs—three of 'em—fried bread—tomatoes . . .

HUMPHREY. Wonderful! (*Then suddenly remembering; excitedly*) And Mrs Carter, do you know what *I'm* going to do?

MRS CARTER. What?

HUMPHREY (*excitedly*) I'm going to—(*pulling up*)—no, no, I can't tell you, but I'm going to do it! (*He claps his hands*)

MRS CARTER (*excitedly*) That's right, sir, you *do*, I don't blame you!

(MRS CARTER *exits into the kitchen.* HUMPHREY *almost jumps around for a moment, clapping his hands. Then he darts to the desk, sits at it, takes paper and pen and prepares to write. He is very excited*)

HUMPHREY (*with pen poised for action; to himself*) Now—er —what was it she said? Ah yes! (*Beginning to write*) Lonely—widow—wishes—to meet——(*Then, realizing his mistake*) No, no, no, no, no! 'T! 't! 't! 't! (*He thinks for a moment*) Ah yes! (*He writes slowly, with pauses for thought*)

(*There now appears at the french windows a strange-looking individual; a man, tall, with a definite 'Beatle' hairdo, a thin beard going round the chin-line from ear to ear, and wearing very dark sunglasses, jeans, a much-studded leather jacket over an outrageous coloured shirt. Slung over his shoulder is a guitar, and a canvas hold-all. Actually, it is* PETER (*'Venture Man'*) Graham—*in disguise.*

PETER, *from just outside the window, looks around the room. He sees Humphrey. After a slight pause he coughs loudly*)

HUMPHREY (*with a guilty start*) Aaah! (*He looks round quickly after slipping the paper he is writing on under the blotter*) Good heavens! (*Moving* L *of the window*) I mean—good morning!

(PETER *quickly slips his guitar into position, and strums single chords on it as he sings*)

PETER (*singing and playing*) 'Yeah! Yeah! Yeah!'

HUMPHREY (*after a slight pause*) I—beg your pardon?

PETER (*again, singing and playing*) 'Yeah! Yeah! Yeah!'

HUMPHREY (*at a loss; after a slight pause*) Er—yes—quite! (*Then as an explanation occurs*) Oh yes, of *course*—I understand! You've called for the *parcels* to take them home to Bulawayo! (*Then raising his voice a little and speaking as if to a foreigner*) They're down—at—the Institute. (*He repeats*) In-sti-tute. It's an English word, meaning . . .

(PETER *comes swiftly into the room, and goes to the kitchen door*)

Oh my goodness!

(PETER *peeps through the kitchen door, then turns and faces Humphrey*)

PETER. Uncle!

HUMPHREY (*in great alarm*) It's a hold-up! Grab and smash! (*He runs to the window and calls*) Help! Help! Police!

(PETER, *with one movement, whips off glasses, beard, which is on elastic, and wig. He is now seen to be a good-looking young man of twenty-seven*)

PETER (*moving* LC) Uncle!

(HUMPHREY *turns, and seeing Peter without his wig etc., gives a little yelp*)

(*Flinging his arms wide*) Your loving nephew!

HUMPHREY. Peter! (*Rushing to him and grabbing his hand and pumping it up and down*) My dear boy! But just now you were . . .

PETER. That's right; disguised!

HUMPHREY (*babbling*) But how . . . ?

PETER. Uncle—you've got to help me!

HUMPHREY. How much?

PETER. No, no! I mean *really* help me.

HUMPHREY (*moving to the desk*) You mean a cheque.

PETER. You've got to *hide* me.

HUMPHREY (*turning*) Hide you? From whom?

PETER. How many women are there in England?

HUMPHREY (*gaping*) I've no idea.

PETER. Neither have I—but that's who you've got to hide me from.

HUMPHREY. All the women in . . . ?

PETER. And one in particular.

HUMPHREY. Oh!

PETER. A crazy cretin who's out to snaffle me.

HUMPHREY. But you're already—er—snaffled. We saw it in the paper. Do you mean you're involved with someone else?

PETER (*wildly*) I'm not involved with anybody—and I'm certainly not going to get involved with Pixe ('I'll Get My Man') Potter!

HUMPHREY (*moving* R *of Peter*) But it says in the papers . . .

PETER (*wildly*) I'm not *going* to marry her! She's trying to trick me into it!

HUMPHREY. But she must have some grounds for thinking . . .

PETER. She has neither the *grounds* nor the *brains* for thinking!

Humphrey (*hesitantly*) You haven't—er—plighted her your troth?

Peter. No, and I haven't taken her up any dark alleys either. Uncle, you should see her!

Humphrey. I have seen her—in the paper.

Peter. Dreadful!

Humphrey (*absently*) Lousy! (*Then quickly*) That's what Lady McAlpine said. And Mrs Carter was equally . . . (*Then suddenly*) Mrs Carter! (*Almost dancing with excitement*) Peter! Mrs Carter must meet you—she's one of your most ardent admirers . . .

Peter (*crossing down* R) Uncle, I don't want to meet any women . . .

Humphrey (*babbling*) Oh but Mrs Carter isn't a woman . . . I mean an ordinary woman; she's . . . she's Mrs Carter. I'll get her!

Peter. No, Uncle, no!

Humphrey. She's only in the kitchen. I'll call her! (*He goes to the kitchen door*)

Peter (*moving up and down*) No, Uncle, please! I know exactly what will happen. It always does! A woman only has to see me and—it gets monotonous.

Humphrey (*calling into the kitchen*) Mrs Carter! Mrs Carter! Surprise! Surprise!

Peter (*quickly*) Uncle, please, never mind about your Mrs Carter. Let me explain about this Pixie horror. You see she's been chasing me for weeks and . . .

(Mrs Carter *appears at the kitchen door.* Peter *continues his speech and does not stop speaking until he goes off*)

—last Saturday night she had the colossal nerve to come round to my flat. She was through the door before I could stop her. So I took her out to the sleaziest restaurant I knew in Soho. A couple of newspaper men happened to spot us, and before I could do anything about it, we'd been photographed, and Pixie—blasted—Potter had practically told 'em we were engaged! (*Then, almost in the same breath, indicating Mrs Carter*) Kitchen?

(*At the same time*)

Mrs Carter (*to Humphrey*) What is it, sir?

Humphrey (*indicating Peter*) Look who's here, Mrs Carter!

(Mrs Carter *sees Peter, gives a loud scream, then calls out* 'My Venture Man! My Lovely!' *She rushes to Peter, gives a moan, spins round and begins falling in a faint.* Peter, *as she is falling, automatically holds out his arms so that she falls into them. He has obviously done this many, many times*

*before. He shows no concern
whatsoever, but lifts her up
into a horizontal position in
his arms and goes on talking
without pause.* HUMPHREY
can only look on aghast)

HUMPHREY *(faintly)* Yes.

PETER *(moving easily towards the kitchen door, carrying Mrs
Carter)* So, you see, Uncle, don't you, what a mess I'm in?

(PETER exits to the kitchen with Mrs Carter. HUMPHREY
*puts his hand to his head, totters to the settee and collapses
into it.* PETER *returns, 'dusting' his hands and still talking)*

PETER *(as he comes through the door)* You see, what's happened now is this——

*(HUMPHREY, the moment Peter comes on, bounds to his
feet again)*

—Pixie's told everybody we're going to be married. And my
life's become absolute hell! I spent all day yesterday answering
the phone. Then this morning at half past seven—half past
seven, mark you—I was awakened by a devil of a din out in the
street. I peeped out of the window and, down below, outside
my door, were about thirty women, yelling and shouting 'Save
our Venture Man'.

HUMPHREY *(babbling)* At half past seven! Thirty women—at
half past seven . . . !

PETER. At *half past eight* there were *two hundred* and thirty!
That setted it! I hopped into my emergency disguise outfit—*(he
indicates his clothes)* sneaked out through the back way and
came straight down here.

HUMPHREY. But—what are you . . . ? Where are you . . . ? If
you stay here, in the village, people will recognize you—everyone watches *Venture Man*, in Stebbington-Fawley. *(Happily)*
You've no idea what *you*, being 'Venture Man', has done for me,
my boy!

PETER *(pacing up and down)*. Oh?

HUMPHREY. Oh yes, indeed! I am no longer just the Vicar of
Stebbington-Fawley, but 'Venture Man's' uncle! And it's made
a great difference to my congregation.

PETER. Yes?

HUMPHREY. Whereas in the past it numbered six—it's now
gone up to nine!

PETER. Look, Uncle, you've got to let me stay here.

HUMPHREY. But if it gets known that you're here, the Vicarage
might be invaded by hordes of women and newspaper men—I'm
sure your Aunt Harriette wouldn't like that.

PETER. I've got to hide somewhere—and I'm damned if I'll
go abroad——

(MRS CARTER, *very shaken, appears at the kitchen door.
She has her hand over her eyes. The same fainting business
is repeated*)

(*Without pause*) I loathe going
abroad. There's no place like
England in the spring, and we
only get it once a year. And
why should I miss it, just because of that little husband-
chaser? I'll see her back in
Liverpool first! And as for
marrying her, well—they may
call me 'Venture Man' but
that's one venture I'm not letting myself in for. I'm keeping
out of her way until I've had
time to get things sorted out
and the way they are right
now, they're going to need
some sorting! (*Then, almost in
the same breath, indicating
Mrs Carter and jerking his
head towards the french windows*) The garden—for a
change?

MRS CARTER (*swaying in the
doorway; feebly*) Vicar!
HUMPHREY (*rushing to her,
alarmed, and standing so that
she cannot see Peter*) Mrs
Carter!
MRS CARTER. I've 'ad a
dream—it must've been! I
dreamt that you called me in
here, and there in front of me
was ... (*Suddenly*) That voice!
(*She pushes Humphrey aside,
sees Peter, screams*) 'It is! It is!'
(*Rushing to Peter*) 'My lovely!'
(*Again she moans, turns and
faints*)

(*Again* PETER *automati-
cally catches her and stands
with her in his arms as he
talks*)

HUMPHREY (*completely dazed*) What? Oh, yes, I suppose—
that is ...
PETER (*overlapping, as he carries Mrs Carter out through the
french windows*) Uncle, do please think very seriously about
letting me stay.

(PETER *exits with Mrs Carter.* HUMPHREY *puts his hand to
his head and collapses into the settee, utterly at sea.* PETER
returns 'dusting' his hands—and talking)

PETER (*moving down* R) Well, have you thought, Uncle?
HUMPHREY (*bounding up*) What? No—no—I haven't. I'm
thinking about Mrs Carter.
PETER. Don't worry about her; she'll come round; that's the
trouble—they always do!
HUMPHREY (*gaping*) But she's seen you. She'll tell everyone
in the village you're here.
PETER. But dammit, where *can* I go?—I've got to hide away
somewhere.
HUMPHREY (*babbling*) Perhaps—a cave in Scotland! If you
remember, Robert Bruce found one!

PETER (*snapping*) Yes! *And* it was spider-ridden! (*Pleading*) Uncle—please—let me stay here. (*Crossing to Humphrey*) I'll keep out of sight, I promise you. All I ask are a bed and food!

HUMPHREY. *Food?* My dear Peter, you don't know what you're talking about! There'll be no food in this house from now on.

PETER. What?

HUMPHREY. No—you see, Harriette has given Mrs Carter notice and she's put me on a diet.

PETER. Who has—Mrs Carter?

HUMPHREY. No, no, no! Harriette! Do you know what she gave me for breakfast this morning?

PETER. What?

HUMPHREY. Straw from Bulawayo!

PETER. Oh, my godfathers! And you stood for that?

HUMPHREY. I did—but I'm not going to! Do you know what I'm going to do?

PETER. What?

HUMPHREY. I'm going to—well never mind. And that reminds me, I have an important letter to finish. Er—will you be passing a pillar-box?

PETER (*moving down* L). Between here and Scotland? It's possible.

HUMPHREY (*crossing* R *to the desk*) Well, sit down a minute while I finish my letter. Then you must be on your way. (*He sits at the desk*)

(MRS BARRINGTON-LOCKE'S *voice is heard close by in the garden*)

MRS BARRINGTON-LOCKE (*off* R; *loudly and agitatedly*) Vicar! Vicar are you there?

HUMPHREY (*leaping up*) Winifred!

PETER. Who?

HUMPHREY. Winifred Barrington-Locke! She . . .

PETER. Look, Uncle, I can't cope with another faint just now!

MRS BARRINGTON-LOCKE (*nearer*) Vicar! Vicar! Where are you?

(HUMPHREY *moves quickly towards the window as* MRS BARRINGTON-LOCKE *appears at it.* PETER *moves towards the stairs. From now to the* CURTAIN *the action and dialogue must be very swift*)

MRS BARRINGTON-LOCKE (*as she enters; in great agitation*) Oh, there you are! Didn't you hear me calling? Quick man, brandy!

HUMPHREY. Brandy?

MRS BARRINGTON-LOCKE. She's dead!

(PETER *is pulled up with a jerk*)

HUMPHREY. *What?* Who is?

MRS BARRINGTON-LOCKE. Your Mrs Carter—stretched out all over Harriette's daffodils—she'll be furious!
HUMPHREY (*babbling*) Not—not dead?

(PETER *moves down* LC, *to the* R *arm of the settee*)

MRS BARRINGTON-LOCKE. In a dead faint! (*Looking into the garden quickly*) Oh, she's moving! Brandy, man, brandy!
HUMPHREY. I'm afraid we haven't . . .
MRS BARRINGTON-LOCKE. Water then! She must have *something* thrown over her! Is there a bucket in the kitchen?
HUMPHREY. I—I—I—well I . . .
MRS BARRINGTON-LOCKE. For heaven's sake! I'll go and see! (*She moves to go to the kitchen, and sees Peter*) What? Who on earth is . . . ?
HUMPHREY (*babbling*) I expect you recognize him, Winifred, he's . . .

(PETER *turns to face Mrs Barrington-Locke and automatically holds out his arms ready for 'the faint'*)

MRS BARRINGTON-LOCKE (*firmly*) Out of my way, young man! This is no time for 'bunny-hugging'! (*And she automatically gives Peter a push which sends him sprawling over the arm of the settee*)

(MRS BARRINGTON-LOCKE *stamps off into the kitchen.* PETER, *the moment he is pushed over, begins to yell loudly*)

PETER (*yelling*) My back! My God! She's broken my back! (*He is struggling to get up, but cannot*)
HUMPHREY (*in alarm*) Peter . . . !
PETER (*yelling*) My back! My back!

(MRS CARTER *appears at the window, very shaken*)

MRS CARTER (*weakly*) Vicar—I . . .
HUMPHREY (*rushing up to her, putting his arm round her, and bleating apprehensively*) Mrs Carter—I beg you . . .

(MRS CARTER'S *eyes light on Peter. She pushes Humphrey aside and totters towards Peter*)

MRS CARTER. It is! It *is!* My 'Venture Man'. *My lovely!*
HUMPHREY. Mrs Carter . . .

Unheeding, MRS CARTER *makes to embrace Peter, but again, overcome with emotion, gives a loud moan, and faints on top of him.* PETER *gives a loud howl of agony, as—*

the CURTAIN *falls*

ACT II

SCENE 1

SCENE—*The same. 10 a.m. the following Thursday.*

When the CURTAIN *rises,* HARRIETTE *is discovered sitting at the desk, reading the 'Daily Mail'. She is obviously annoyed at what she is reading. She 'Tut-tuts!' occasionally, and gives vent to irritable 'Oh's'. Then, unconsciously crushing the paper into a somewhat mangled mess, she move. to the french windows and calls out.*

HARRIETTE (*calling sharply*) Arthur!

(*Almost immediately,* HUMPHREY *appears at the windows. He is carrying a pair of shears*)

HUMPHREY (*anxiously*) Yes, Harriette? Is it the post?

HARRIETTE (*exasperated*) It is *not* the post! It's (*holding out the paper*) all this nonsense about Peter. (*She moves up* C)

HUMPHREY (*not listening*) He's very late! (*He follows Harriette*)

HARRIETTE. Peter?

HUMPHREY. The postman!

HARRIETTE (*still exasperated*) Why all this anxiety about the post? Are you expecting something special?

HUMPHREY (*trying to be casual*) No, no. (*Moving to the desk*) But I am expecting a letter. Nothing—er—special—that is—er . . . (*Guiltily*) What were you saying, Harriette? It was nonsense, of course.

HARRIETTE (*sharply*) What?

HUMPHREY (*quickly*) I mean—you said something *about* nonsense.

HARRIETTE. Yes! All this tarra-diddle about Peter's disappearance in the papers.

HUMPHREY. But you read that before breakfast.

HARRIETTE (*sitting on the* L *arm of the armchair; tartly*) And I shall probably read it again before lunch! It's quite ridiculous! There wouldn't be more fuss if the Prime Minister had disappeared.

HUMPHREY (*quietly*) Far *less*, I imagine!

HARRIETTE. And I feel terrible—reading all this 'Where is he? Where is he?' rubbish and knowing full well he's in our second-best bedroom!

HUMPHREY. Well—his back . . .

B   29

HARRIETTE. There's nothing wrong with his back. It's just an excuse for him to hide away here in the Vicarage.

HUMPHREY. Oh, I hardly think . . .

HARRIETTE. That is an overstatement, Arthur; you don't think at all! Why has Peter resolutely refused to let the doctor see him?

HUMPHREY. Mrs Carter is doing him more good than any doctor. Three times a day she's massaged his back.

HARRIETTE (*snapping*) You don't have to tell me that. The whole house reeks of wintergreen!

(*There is a bump on the kitchen door, and* MRS CARTER *enters carrying a tray loaded with coffee-pot, milk jug, covered dishes and all that would be required for a hearty breakfast. She makes straight for the staircase*)

HUMPHREY (*almost the moment he hears the bump; turning*) The post? (*Then, seeing it isn't*) Oh!

HARRIETTE (*rising; tartly*) Mrs Carter . . .

MRS CARTER (*firmly*) Sorry. Can't stop! (*Moving upstairs*) 'Is breakfast! Got to get it to 'im while it's 'ot!

HARRIETTE (*determined to speak*) Mrs Carter . . .

MRS CARTER (*determined not to be spoken to*) Sorry an' all that, but . . .

(MRS CARTER *exits along the landing*)

HARRIETTE (*fuming*) One thing is certain. The moment Peter leaves this house, that woman leaves too.

HUMPHREY (*almost grinning*) What is more certain, Harriette, she won't leave until he *does*. Er—have you finished with the *Daily Mail*, Harriette? I have *The Times* here if you'd like it.

HARRIETTE (*handing him the 'Daily Mail'; shortly*) Not at the moment. By the way—we never solved the mystery of yesterday's *Times*, did we?

HUMPHREY (*embarrassed*) Er—no! (*He moves down* R)

HARRIETTE. Most extraordinary. You had it at the breakfast table, and then—somehow—it just disappeared!

HUMPHREY. Er—yes.

(MRS CARTER *appears on the landing*)

MRS CARTER (*happily*) There! That's got 'im settled—till I do 'is back, bless 'im!

(*There is a ring at the front door bell*)

HUMPHREY (*at once*) Ah! That may be the post. I'll . . . (*He is about to cross to the arch* L)

HARRIETTE (*restraining him with a gesture*) Arthur! Mrs Carter, will you see who it is, please!

MRS CARTER (*after a 'look' at Harriette*) Yes'm!

(Mrs Carter *exits down* l)

Harriette (*to Humphrey*) We *do* pay Mrs Carter to attend to *our* needs as well, Arthur.

Humphrey. Er—quite. I just thought . . . (*He moves to his desk*)

Mrs Carter (*off; in amazement*) Oh my Gawd . . . !

Harriette (*tartly*) Now what . . . ?

Mrs Carter (*off*) What? What's that? . . . Yes, well 'ang on a minute, will you? Oh my Gawd!

Harriette. What *is* going on out there?

(Mrs Carter *comes in, staggering under the weight of a well-filled post office mailbag*)

Mrs Carter (*as she enters*) Oh my Gawd! (*She puffs*)

Humphrey. Goodness gracious! What . . . ?

Harriette. What on earth . . . ?

Mrs Carter (*gasping*) The post! (*She staggers* lc)

Harriette. *What?*

Mrs Carter. Special delivery; come by van. All letters he says. And there'll be another batch this afternoon.

Harriette (*gaping*) But they—they *can't* be ours!

Mrs Carter (*panting*) That postman'll 'ear my tongue if they aren't!

Harriette (*suddenly*) Arthur! Don't you see! They must be Peter's!

Humphrey (*babbling*) Peter's, but . . .

Harriette (*firmly*) They've found out where he is! This must all be—'fan-mail' or whatever they call it.

Mrs Carter (*trying to interrupt*) 'Scuse me . . .

Harriette (*more firmly*) Arthur! This settles it! Peter must go! We're not going to have the house littered with letters every post . . .

Mrs Carter (*again trying to interrupt*) 'Scuse me . . .

Harriette (*snapping*) Mrs Carter, do you mind? I am speaking!

Mrs Carter (*snapping back*) And I'm *tryin'* to! That postman outside says he wants his bag back an' will we jump to it cos' 'e's in a hurry!

Harriette. Well, let him have it.

Mrs Carter (*up-ending the bag*) Right!

Harriette (*wildly*) Not on the floor . . . !

(*But* Harriette *is too late.* Mrs Carter *has shaken the bag and at least three hundred letters fall to the floor*)

Mrs Carter (*gaping at them*) Oh my Gawd!

(Humphrey *moves* r *of the letters*)

HARRIETTE (*turning on Humphrey*) You will speak to Peter about this, Arthur, and if you don't I *will*!

(*An annoyed voice—male—is heard off down* L)

VOICE (*off*) Oi! Wot about my bag?

HARRIETTE (*wildly*) For heaven's sake take the man his wretched bag. And tell him we don't want to see another!

MRS CARTER (*moving to the arch with the bag*) Stone the crows!

(MRS CARTER *exits down* L)

HARRIETTE (*fuming*) Do you realize the time *we've* got to waste—searching for *our* letters amongst all these? (*She goes down on her knees by the pile of letters. She picks up several letters—one at a time—and throws them down again without consciously looking at them, as she lectures Humphrey*) And I suppose this is going to happen every day while Peter's here! We're going to be snowed under with letters—and not only with letters, because you know what's going to happen next, don't you?

HUMPHREY. Er—no.

HARRIETTE (*picking up another letter and looking at it as she speaks*) For goodness' sake, Arthur, use your brains! (*Then holding a letter out to him; uninterested*) This is for you.

HUMPHREY (*taking the letter quickly*) Oh!

HARRIETTE (*picking up another letter and looking at it as she goes on talking*) If they know where Peter is—and they obviously do . . . (*Breaking off and handing him a letter*) And this.

HUMPHREY (*somewhat surprised*) Oh! Another! (*He takes the letter*)

HARRIETTE (*picking up another letter and resuming about Peter*) The next thing that's going to happen is—we shall . . . (*Again breaking off and handing him a letter*) And this.

HUMPHREY. Goodness gracious! (*Taking the letter*)

HARRIETTE (*picking up another letter*) We shall have the Vicarage swarming with reporters, fans, television cameras and heaven knows what else besides! (*Breaking off again and handing him a letter*) And this.

HUMPHREY (*taking the letter*) Oh my . . . !

HARRIETTE (*picking up another letter*) Well, I tell you now, Arthur . . . (*She suddenly stops talking, with a puzzled look on her face, and concentrates on the letters. She looks hard at the one she is holding, then picks up another, and another, and another. She then dives her hand to the bottom of the pile and brings up another letter, and looks at it. In an almost croaking voice*) Arthur!

HUMPHREY (*preoccupied; studying the envelopes in his hand*) Yes, Harriette?

HARRIETTE. These letters! They're not Peter's!
HUMPHREY. Not?
HARRIETTE. They're *yours!*
HUMPHREY (*almost leaping into the air*) *What?*
HARRIETTE. *Yours!*
HUMPHREY. All of them?
HARRIETTE (*scooping up some letters with both hands*) Look!

(MRS BARRINGTON-LOCKE'S *voice is heard off down* L *talking with* MRS CARTER)

MRS BARRINGTON-LOCKE (*off*) Morning, Mrs Carter!
MRS CARTER (*off*) Morning!
HARRIETTE. Winifred! She would *arrive* just at this moment.
Arthur . . . !
MRS BARRINGTON-LOCKE (*off; almost overlapping*) Vicar in?
MRS CARTER (*off*) Straight through.
HARRIETTE (*still on her knees*) Arthur—quickly—all these
letters—what does it mean?
HUMPHREY (*limply*) They'll have to be answered!

(MRS BARRINGTON-LOCKE *sails in from* L)

MRS BARRINGTON-LOCKE (*breezily*) Ah! Here you . . . (*Seeing
Harriette on her knees*) What the devil are *you* doing, old girl?
Praying?
HARRIETTE (*weakly*) Winifred . . .
MRS BARRINGTON-LOCKE. Morning, Vicar. Want a word with
you! (*Then to Harriette*) Oh, I see! Spring-cleaning! Mind if I
sit down? Feet giving me hell this morning! (*She sits on the
settee*) And now—what have you been up to, Vicar?
HUMPHREY (*puzzled*) What have I been . . . ?
MRS BARRINGTON-LOCKE. Outside your gate just now, I passed
Mrs—er—er—'what's it?', and Mrs—er—'thingummy'—*you*
know them—and as I was passing I heard Mrs—er—'what's it' say
to Mrs 'thingummy': 'Have you heard about the Vicar?' It was
all I could do to stop myself stopping and saying: 'No. What?'
—but I didn't. When I turned in here, one of 'em gave a hell
of a roar of laughter and said to the other, 'Think *she's* goin' to
try her luck?'
HARRIETTE (*rising*) What on earth could she mean?
MRS BARRINGTON-LOCKE. That's what I'd like to know.
Vicar . . . ?

(MRS CARTER *enters from down* L, *and makes for the stairs*)

MRS CARTER (*very conspiratorially*) 'Scuse me. (*On the stairs,
to Humphrey*) Just going up to . . . (*She points, indicating
'Peter'*)
HUMPHREY (*embarrassed*) Oh—er—yes . . .

MRS CARTER. To . . . (*She rubs one hand vigorously across the palm of the other, indicating 'rub his back'*)

HARRIETTE (*also embarrassed; quickly*) Thank you, Mrs Carter!

MRS CARTER. Don't mention it. (*With great sincerity*) It's a pleasure!

(MRS BARRINGTON-LOCKE *looks from one to the other, distinctly puzzled*)

(*To Humphrey*) Finished with the paper?

HUMPHREY. Er—paper?

MRS CARTER. For . . . (*Again jabbing her finger, meaning 'for Peter'*)

HUMPHREY (*picking up 'The Times' from the desk*) Oh—er—yes. (*Very aware of Mrs Barrington-Locke*) Here's *The Times'*. You—you'll find it very interesting reading, Mrs Carter.

MRS CARTER. Thank you, sir. (*She goes to the stairs and turns*) Will you be up shortly?

(MRS BARRINGTON-LOCKE *gives a big start*)

HUMPHREY (*aware of this*) I—I . . . We'll see, Mrs Carter. We'll see!

(MRS CARTER *exits upstairs.* HUMPHREY *moves to the desk. There is an awkward pause*)

MRS BARRINGTON-LOCKE (*heavily*) I don't get it!

HARRIETTE (*apprehensively*) Get what?

MRS BARRINGTON-LOCKE. How you can afford to pay that woman whatever-it-is-you-do-pay-her-an-hour, to go upstairs and sit—where I *presume* she's going to sit—reading *The Times*!

HARRIETTE (*babbling*) Well—I—I . . .

MRS BARRINGTON-LOCKE (*to Humphrey*) And as for you joining her 'shortly'—well, we won't go into that!

HARRIETTE. Winifred!

MRS BARRINGTON-LOCKE (*explosively*) What the hell is going on in this house?

(*The telephone rings*)

HUMPHREY. I'll take it, Harriette!

MRS BARRINGTON-LOCKE (*still 'exploding'*) And don't tell me there isn't something going on, because . . .

HUMPHREY (*to Mrs Barrington-Locke; phone in hand*) Sssssssh! (*into the phone*) The Vicarage, Stebbington-Fawley, the Vicar speaking . . . (*Sitting*) *What* name? . . . Mrs Annie Sparkes . . . (*To Harriette*) Do we know a Mrs Annie Sparkes, Harriette?

HARRIETTE (*shortly*) We do not! (*She sits* RC)

HUMPHREY (*into the phone*) Well—er—what can I do for

you, Mrs Sparkes? . . , What was that? . . . Good heavens! (*To Harriette*) She says to begin with I can call her 'Annie'!

MRS BARRINGTON-LOCKE. Well, I'll be . . . !

HUMPHREY (*into the phone*) Er—where are you speaking from —Annie?

HARRIETTE (*horrified*) Arthur!

HUMPHREY (*after listening*) . . . Chorlton-cum-Hardy . . .

MRS BARRINGTON-LOCKE. Where the hell's that?

HUMPHREY (*into the phone*) Where the hell's that?

HARRIETTE. Arthur!

HUMPHREY (*into the phone*) . . . From a call-box . . . Well— er—we mustn't waste time then, must we? What was it you wanted to say to me? . . . You're a *widow* . . .

HARRIETTE (*hissing*) Who *is* this woman?

HUMPHREY (*into the phone; sympathetically*) . . . With only two children. (*Slight pause*) Did you want *more*? . . .

HARRIETTE. Arthur!

HUMPHREY (*startled*) Good heavens! (*To the others*) She says 'Yes, please!'

(HARRIETTE *and* MRS BARRINGTON-LOCKE *give gasps of horror*)

(*Into the phone; puzzled*) Well, I could put you in touch with the 'Missions to Seamen' . . .

HARRIETTE (*with a wail*) Arthur! (*She buries her face in her hands*)

HUMPHREY (*into the phone*) . . . What was that? . . . You don't *like* sailors. You prefer—parso—Oh! (*he now realizes the reason for the call. He shows intense embarrassment, with scared looks towards Harriette as he babbles*) Oh but—er—madam— Annie—I'm afraid . . . No, no it's impossible—out of the ques- tion . . . No, no, *please!* There would be no point in my coming to Chorlton-cum-Hardy . . . No . . . No. I—I . . . (*With relief*) Oh! There go the pips . . . (*Frantically*) No, no, you mustn't put another five sixpences in . . . No, Annie. . . . *No!* Waste of money. You should never have phoned. I don't know where you got my number. I . . . Good-bye! . . . Yes, yes—forever! Goodbye! (*He almost collapses over the phone as he replaces the receiver*) Oh my goodness! Oh my goodness! (*He produces a handkerchief and wipes his brow*)

HARRIETTE. And now, Arthur, will you kindly explain?

HUMPHREY (*staggering to his feet; considerably shaken*) What, my dear?

HARRIETTE. What was that all about? And who was that woman?

HUMPHREY (*almost groping his way around*) What? Oh, it was —er—a Mrs Annie Sparkes from Chorlton-cum-Hardy. (*He strides over the pile of letters*) She—she wants some more

children, apparently—and she thought I might ... Oh my goodness! (*Wiping his brow again*) Er—will you excuse me if I take
a turn round the garden? I'm feeling slightly—er—er ...

MRS BARRINGTON-LOCKE (*pointedly*) You *look* it!

HUMPHREY (*moving towards the stairs*) Yes, I—I—a little air
—in the garden ... (*He is mounting the stairs*) The garden ... !
(*He realizes his mistake*) Oh! er—I ... (*He comes downstairs,
totters over to the window, again striding over the letters. As
he reaches the window; looking out*) Ah! Here it is! (*He turns
and looks apprehensively at the ladies*)

(HARRIETTE *and* MRS BARRINGTON-LOCKE *are watching him
keenly.* HUMPHREY *dashes out through the windows*)

MRS BARRINGTON-LOCKE (*very big*) *Well!*

HARRIETTE (*feebly*) Yes.

MRS BARRINGTON-LOCKE (*rising and moving to the window*)
Either your brother is going 'nuts', or he's up to something.
Which do you think it is?

HARRIETTE. Both!

MRS BARRINGTON-LOCKE (*looking out*) D'you think he's safe
out there on his own?

(MRS CARTER *appears on the stairs, very excited*)

HARRIETTE (*rising; almost wildly*) Leave him out there.
Don't ...

(HARRIETTE *becomes aware of* MRS CARTER *signalling
frantically*)

What ... ?

(MRS CARTER *gestures and 'mouths' silently that Peter—
upstairs—is coming down*)

(*Getting the message*) Oh no!

(MRS CARTER *nods her head vigorously.* MRS BARRINGTON-
LOCKE *turns and sees this*)

(*To Mrs Carter, with her back to Mrs Barrington-Locke*) Can't
you ... (*She gestures and 'mouths': 'Go up and tell him there's
someone here!' On the 'someone here' she turns, pointing to
Mrs Barrington-Locke, then realizes* MRS BARRINGTON-LOCKE
*is watching her. Trying very unsuccessfully to pull herself to-
gether*) Er—thank you, Mrs Carter. That will be all! (*She
collapses into the armchair*)

MRS CARTER. Yes'm!

(MRS CARTER *exits into the kitchen*)

MRS BARRINGTON-LOCKE (*striding firmly into the room*)

Strikes me the Vicar isn't the only one who's slightly *off the beam*!

HARRIETTE (*weakly*) Winifred . . . !

MRS BARRINGTON-LOCKE. In fact, if you ask me, I'd say there isn't a damn person in this house who's *on* it!

HARRIETTE (*still weakly*) Winifred, would you think me very rude if I asked you to go now?

MRS BARRINGTON-LOCKE (*definitely*) Yes! (*She sits on the settee*)

HARRIETTE. I am—a—a little—er—put out this morning.

(PETER *peeps cautiously in from the landing*)

MRS BARRINGTON-LOCKE. A *little?*

HARRIETTE (*rising*) You see . . . (*She looks unconsciously towards the staircase, sees Peter's head, and gasps*) Peter!

(PETER *backs instantly*)

MRS BARRINGTON-LOCKE (*whose back is to the stairs*) What?

HARRIETTE (*lamely*) I didn't say anything.

MRS. BARRINGTON-LOCKE (*accusingly*) Yes, you did; you said 'Peter!'

HARRIETTE. Did I? I must have been thinking about him. I —I've thought about him a lot lately.

MRS BARRINGTON-LOCKE (*puzzled*) Who? *Saint* Peter?

HARRIETTE. No, no. Our nephew, Peter.

MRS BARRINGTON-LOCKE (*off-handed*) Oh, you mean the television bloke! But why should you suddenly think about him? Is it his birthday or something?

HARRIETTE. No, no. (*Acidly, with a sly look towards the stairs*) Though I wish him *many happy returns to—to television!*

(PETER'S *face comes round the staircase arch for a second. He gives Harriette a beaming smile, and a little wave of the hand.* HARRIETTE *starts—then looks to Mrs Barrington-Locke*)

MRS BARRINGTON-LOCKE. Harriette, old girl, I don't know what the hell you're talking about, and I'm damn sure you don't.

HARRIETTE (*tottering to the armchair and sitting*) But, surely you've read about him in the papers?

MRS BARRINGTON-LOCKE. No, I haven't. The only things I read in the papers are 'Births, Marriages and Deaths' and the racing tips.

HARRIETTE. But—they were on about him on television last night.

MRS BARRINGTON-LOCKE. You know damn well I haven't got a television. Wouldn't give it house room! What were they on about.

HARRIETTE. Well—he's—he's disappeared.

MRS BARRINGTON-LOCKE. I expect thousands of viewers are thankful for that!

(PETER's *face again comes round the staircase arch—with thumb to nose—at Mrs Barrington-Locke's back*)

HARRIETTE. He should have attended an important conference yesterday—about a new—er—*Venture Man* series, but he—he didn't turn up. He's disappeared completely. Apparently the whole country is on the look out for him.

MRS BARRINGTON-LOCKE. *Is* it? Well, *I'm* not! Wouldn't know the feller if I saw him.

HARRIETTE. You wouldn't?

MRS BARRINGTON-LOCKE. No!

HARRIETTE. Oh!

PETER (*peeping round*) Oh! (*He withdraws*)

(HARRIETTE *gives a little start*)

MRS BARRINGTON-LOCKE (*looking up*) This room developing an echo? I still don't see what all this rigmarole about your nephew disappearing has to do with the way the Vicar—and you—are behaving.

HARRIETTE. Well—you see . . .

MRS BARRINGTON-LOCKE. I've just told you I *don't* see!

HARRIETTE. Well . . .

(PETER *appears on the stairs and runs lightly down them. Since last putting his face round the staircase arch he has put on a pair of horn-rimmed glasses. His hair is parted down the middle. He wears a clerical grey suit and a parson's collar and bib*)

PETER (*as he runs down the stairs; in a slightly parsonic voice*) Good morning, dear people!

(HARRIETTE *rises and spins round.* MRS BARRINGTON-LOCKE *leaps to her feet*)

(*To Mrs Barrington-Locke*) No—no, please. I beg you—don't ascend. Do be—parked. (*He puts her on the settee again*)

MRS BARRINGTON-LOCKE (*goggling*) What? Who? Harriette . . . ?

PETER (*going to the window*) Lovely, lovely morning, wouldn't you say? And look at those flowers! Those daffo-down-dillies! Wouldn't Wordsworth have gone crackers about them? What was it he . . . ? Ah yes! (*Quoting*)

'I wandered lonely as a cloud
  That floats on high o'er vales and hills,
  When all at once I saw a crowd
  A host of golden daffodils!' (*Then*) Yippee!

MRS BARRINGTON-LOCKE (*still goggling*) Harriette . . . !

PETER (*coming back into the room*) Forgive me, Miss Humphrey. I got carried away. I do occasionally! (*Seeing the letters on the floor*) Oh, Miss Humphrey, you never told me!

HARRIETTE. What?

PETER (*singing*) 'Happy Birthday to you!
         Happy Birthday to you!
         Happy Birthday, Miss Humphrey—
         Happy Birthday to you!'

HARRIETTE. I—I—I . . . (*She is at a complete loss for words*)

PETER. Ah! The old throat troubling you again? (*Waggling a finger at her*) I've told you before—you talk too much! (*Then to Mrs Barrington-Locke*) May I make so bold as to introduce myself? The name is—er—(*after sniffing twice*) Wintergreen.

MRS BARRINGTON-LOCKE. Wintergreen?

PETER. *Percival* Wintergreen. (*He squeezes on the settee* R *of Mrs Barrington-Locke*)

MRS BARRINGTON-LOCKE (*babbling*) Percival . . . ?

PETER. 'Percy' to my friends. (*He kisses her hand*)

MRS BARRINGTON-LOCKE (*babbling*) But I didn't know—Harriette didn't tell me . . . (*To Harriette*) You never mentioned you had a visitor, Harriette?

PETER. Ah! dear faithful Miss Humphrey.

MRS BARRINGTON-LOCKE. What?

PETER. I asked her *not* to. You see, I am—er—in *retreat*.

MRS BARRINGTON-LOCKE. What from?

PETER. Oh—er—the hurly-burly of daily life.

MRS BARRINGTON-LOCKE (*growling*) You'll find damn little hurly-burly in Stebbington-Fawley!

PETER. Furthermore, and notwithstanding. I am here to receive—'Instruction'.

MRS BARRINGTON-LOCKE. Who from?

PETER. Er—*Mr* Humphrey.

MRS BARRINGTON-LOCKE. Then heaven help you!

PETER. We *are* hoping for a little aid from that quarter.

HARRIETTE (*at bursting point*) Pe . . . (*She is about to say 'Peter'*)

PETER (*rising quickly to* C) 'Percy,' Miss Humphrey, I beg you! After all we *have* known each other—a day or two.

(MRS CARTER *comes from the kitchen and moves* C. *The moment she comes on she has eyes for no one but Peter. She stands close to him, giggles happily.* PETER *giggles back*)

MRS CARTER (*generally*) Was you wanting coffee?

PETER (*generally*) Er—was we?

(MRS CARTER *gives him a dig in the ribs and giggles.* PETER *returns the dig in the ribs.* MRS BARRINGTON-LOCKE *watches this*)

HARRIETTE (*reluctantly*) Winifred, would you care for . . . ?

MRS BARRINGTON-LOCKE. Not for me, thanks.

MRS CARTER (*to Harriette*) How about you'm?

HARRIETTE. No thank you!

MRS CARTER (*adoringly to Peter*) You will, won't you?

PETER (*gazing 'adoringly' at her*) Will I?

MRS CARTER. Course you will!

PETER. Since you insist, I *will* have a—soupçon.

MRS CARTER (*moving to the kitchen door*) You won't, you know—you'll 'ave a 'Nescaff'.

(MRS CARTER *exits to the kitchen*)

MRS BARRINGTON-LOCKE (*rising; distinctly puzzled*) Yes—well —if you are in—retreat, Mr Wintergreen, you won't want a lot of women fussing round you.

PETER. No! (*Then quickly*) But then—you're not a *lot*, are you? I mean—(*after a glance at her figure*) there may be a lot *of* you, but . . .

MRS BARRINGTON-LOCKE (*giggling*) I'll wish you good morning, young man!

PETER (*breezily, waving a 'paw'*) Good morning, old girl— er—dear lady!

MRS BARRINGTON-LOCKE. 'Bye, Harriette! (*Moving to the french windows*) No need to see me out.

HARRIETTE (*rising and following her*) Oh, but . . .

MRS BARRINGTON-LOCKE (*after a look towards Peter's back; in a lower voice*) And, Harriette . . .

HARRIETTE. Yes?

MRS BARRINGTON-LOCKE. If (*with a nod of her head towards Peter*) that young devil's a *parson*——

(HARRIETTE *is about to speak*)

(*Sweeping on*)—it's a pity there aren't a damn sight more *like* him!

(MRS BARRINGTON-LOCKE *exits through the window*)

HARRIETTE. Oh! (*She turns, fuming, and barks*) Peter!

PETER (*turning and wagging a finger at her*) 'Percy', Auntie, 'Percy'! Percy *Wintergreen*! Wintergreen! (*He holds his nose*) Phew! I shall go to my grave smelling of wintergreen!

HARRIETTE (*moving down* R) Don't talk nonsense. But I'll tell you where you *will* go—out of this house!

PETER. No, Auntie, no!

HARRIETTE. You will pack your things and leave immediately!

PETER (*with a hand to his back*) My back! Ooh! My back! (*He hobbles around*)

HARRIETTE. There's nothing wrong with your back now—and I doubt if there ever was.

PETER. But, Auntie—dear Auntie—you can't turn me out to face all those angry women on the look-out for me all over England—to say nothing of Pixie—'I'll Get My Man'—Potter!

HARRIETTE. You are not staying here in—(*pointing*) that ridiculous outfit.

PETER (*in mock horror*) Ridiculous! A parson's collar ridiculous? Auntie, I shall tell the Bishop about you!

(HUMPHREY *comes running in from the garden to* C)

HUMPHREY (*as he comes in*) Harriette! Harriette! What *do* you think?

PETER. She thinks a parson's collar's ridiculous.

HUMPHREY. Well, so do I! (*Then blinking at Peter*) What . . . ? Oh! Who—er—good morning! (*Holding out his hand*) I am the Vicar of Stebbington-Fawley.

PETER (*shaking Humphrey's hand*) And I am the curate of Merton-on-Creek!

HUMPHREY. Good heavens! You're Peter!

PETER. Good heavens! So I am!

HUMPHREY. But what . . . ? (*Pointing to Peter's collar*) Why . . . ?

HARRIETTE (*grimly*) He thinks he's going to stay on here, disguised as a parson.

HUMPHREY (*delighted*) But that's a wonderful idea! Very subtle! You can read the lessons on Sunday!

HARRIETTE. *Arthur!*

HUMPHREY (*abashed*) Well, no—perhaps not! (*Then brightly*) But he can go round with the collection plate. (*An afterthought, to Peter*) It won't take long! (*Then looking at it*) Oh! I like your collar, Peter!

PETER. Do you, Uncle! How nice!

HUMPHREY. Very nice! *So* much nicer than mine. Where did you get it?

PETER. Your collar-box.

HARRIETTE (*fuming*) Ooh! (*Moving* R *of Humphrey*) Arthur! What was it you came in to say?

HUMPHREY. Er—did I come in to say something? Now what could it have been?

PETER. Grace? 'For what we are about to . . .'

HUMPHREY. No, no, I remember! Harriette, I'm going to have my photograph taken.

HARRIETTE. Your . . .

HUMPHREY. Most extraordinary! I was in the potting shed— (*to Peter*) it's near the road, you know.

PETER. No, I didn't—but thanks for telling me.

HUMPHREY. And I heard a man asking old Simpson, the road-man, if this was the Vicarage, and when Simpson told him it was, this man asked him if he thought I was at home because he

wanted to take my photograph! So I thought I'd better slip back
quietly and put my best jacket on.

HARRIETTE. But why should anyone want to photograph you?

HUMPHREY. I can't think. He told Simpson he was from the
National Press Agency—whoever they are.

PETER. National Press? But good God—I mean my goodness
gracious me! That means your photograph's going to appear in
the papers, Uncle!

HUMPHREY. What? Oh no!

HARRIETTE. Arthur, in heaven's name what have you been up
to?

HUMPHREY. Nothing—nothing—only . . .

HARRIETTE. Only what?

HUMPHREY (*babbling*) But the newspapers couldn't possibly
be interested in that.

HARRIETTE (*insistently*) In what, man, what?

(*There is a ring at the front door bell*)

HUMPHREY (*with a little yelp*) That's him! He's at the door!
Harriette, do I have to go and put my best jacket on?

HARRIETTE. You will stay where you are, and keep quiet!
Leave this to me!

(HARRIETTE *marches off down* L)

PETER (*wagging a finger*) Now come on, Uncle; confess to
nephew. What have you . . . ?

HUMPHREY (*frantically*) Ssssh! (*He runs to arch* L *and stands
listening*)

PETER. Eh?

HUMPHREY. I want to hear what Harriette is going to say.

HARRIETTE (*off*) Not today, thank you.

(*There is a loud door slam off* L)

PETER (*hearing this*) She's said it! Look out, Uncle!

(HUMPHREY *comes quickly away from the arch.* PETER *puts
his arms round him protectingly.* HARRIETTE *enters* L)

HARRIETTE (*grimly*) And that is that!

PETER. It sounded like it. Was it the photographer?

HARRIETTE. It was.

PETER. What did you say to him?

HARRIETTE. Nothing!

PETER. Very wise.

HARRIETTE. I just shut the door in his face!

PETER. Very *un*-wise. The Press don't enjoy having doors shut
in their faces.

HUMPHREY. Oh dear, oh dear! (*He puts his hand to his head*)

(MRS CARTER *enters with a cup of coffee on a tray*)

MRS CARTER (*approaching Peter*) Here we are! I 'ave sugared it, my lovely.

HUMPHREY (*taking the coffee cup automatically*) Thank you, my darling. Just what I need! (*He swallows some coffee instantly*)

(*The telephone rings*)

(*In alarm*) Oh my . . . ! (*Handing the cup and saucer to Peter*) You can finish that, my boy! (*He moves to the desk*)

HARRIETTE. Arthur! If it's that woman again . . . !

PETER. Good Lord! Is *that* it? Has Uncle got a woman?

HARRIETTE (*furiously*) Peter! How dare you!

MRS CARTER (*turning on Harriette*) Don't you snap at *him*! 'E asked a reasonable question, an' 'e wants a reasonable answer!

HUMPHREY (*into the phone*) Hello . . . Hello . . . ?

HARRIETTE. Mrs Carter will you please leave us!

MRS CARTER. I will. But let me catch you gettin' at my lovely . . . !

(MRS CARTER *exits into the kitchen*)

HUMPHREY (*into the phone*) The Vicarage, Stebbington-Fawley; the Vicar speaking . . . Who? . . . The *Daily* . . . ? (*To the others*) It's the *Daily Mirror*!

HARRIETTE. Arthur!

HUMPHREY (*into the phone*) Will I *what*? . . . 'Story'? . . . But . . . (*To the others*) They—they want me to tell them a story! I don't quite . . . (*Into the phone*) Do you mean a Bible story?

PETER. *Not* the *Daily Mirror*!

HUMPHREY (*into the phone; bewildered*) If so, I could tell you about Joseph and his coat of many colours . . . Oh, you know that one!

PETER. Ask 'em if they know the one about the young lady from Gloucester!

HUMPHREY (*into the phone*) Do you know that one about . . . ?

(HARRIETTE *rushes across to the desk, takes the receiver from Humphrey and slams it down on its cradle*)

HARRIETTE (*fuming*) Get away from this phone!

HUMPHREY. But, Harriette . . . !

HARRIETTE. If you don't get away from this phone I shall scream!

PETER (*quickly*) Oh, Uncle, *please* get away from that phone!

(HUMPHREY *moves quickly away from the desk to* C)

HARRIETTE. And now, Arthur, no more shilly-shallying! I want to know what all this is about. *Why* did that woman phone you from Chorlton-cum-wherever-it-was?

HUMPHREY (*limply*) Hardy.

HARRIETTE. *Why* did that man want to take your photograph?

HUMPHREY. I—I—Harriette...!

HARRIETTE (*pressing on relentlessly*) Why did the *Daily Mirror* want a story?

PETER. Auntie, you *are* inquisitive this morning! 'Why, why, why!'

HARRIETTE (*with a big gesture*) And what is the meaning of all these letters? (*Pointing to them*)

PETER (*looking at the pile*) Good Lord! Are these all yours, Uncle?

HARRIETTE. I am waiting, Arthur.

PETER. Auntie's waiting, Uncle.

HUMPHREY (*babbling*) They're—they're just in answer to an —an appeal I made.

HARRIETTE. An appeal? Do you mean for the 'Beetle Fund'?

PETER. What? Don't tell me 'the Beatles' are broke already!

HARRIETTE (*snapping at him*) The death-watch beetles—in the church.

PETER. Sor-ry!

HARRIETTE. Well, Arthur.

HUMPHREY (*still babbling*) No, no! It wasn't for the 'Beetle Fund'—exactly.

HARRIETTE. Then what was it for—exactly?

HUMPHREY (*wretchedly*) A wife!

HARRIETTE. *A wife?*

PETER. A *wife?*

HARRIETTE. You—you appealed for ...? (*Collapsing into the desk-chair; beginning quietly, but her voice getting higher as she goes on*) I don't believe it! *I don't believe it!* I DON'T BELIEVE IT! (*She begins to whimper hysterically*)

PETER. Uncle, 'Doubting Thomasina' doesn't believe it. And I must say it takes a bit of swallowing! Where did you make this—appeal?

HUMPHREY (*wretchedly*) In *The Times.*

HARRIETTE (*with a yelp*) *The Times?*

HUMPHREY. The Personal Column; yesterday.

HARRIETTE. You mean you—you *advertised*——

HUMPHREY (*nodding his head; wretchedly*) Huh-huh!

HARRIETTE. —for *a wife?*

PETER. Huh-huh!

HARRIETTE. And you—you gave your *name* and *address?*

HUMPHREY. Well, if I hadn't, how could anyone have applied for—the post?

HARRIETTE (*hammering her clenched fists on the side of the chair*) Ooooh!

PETER. You could have used a *nom-de-plume*, Uncle. 'Love-starved bachelor' or—er—something.

HARRIETTE. What did you say in this advertisement?

HUMPHREY. Say?

HARRIETTE. How did you word it, for heaven's sake?

HUMPHREY. Now let me think! Oh, there's no need to! I kept a copy. *(Moving to the desk)* I put it somewhere——

(HARRIETTE beats her fists on the chair again)

—somewhere where you wouldn't find it, Harriette. Now where ... Ah yes! *(He turns up a corner of the mat by the desk and produces a piece of paper)* Here it is. Shall I read it to you?

PETER *(taking it from him)* Let me. *(Reading)* 'Bachelor clergyman would like to meet lady who would love, cherish and cook ...' Oh my godfathers!

HARRIETTE *(wailing)* Arthur!

PETER *(reading)* 'Love, cherish and cook in a charming country Vicarage; electric oven; indoor sanitation; *single beds if desirable*'!

HARRIETTE *(with a shriek) Arthur!*

PETER *(still reading)* Application by letter only. No callers. The Reverend Arthur Humphrey, The Vicarage, Stebbington-Fawley, near Badcaster, Sussex.

HUMPHREY *(somewhat anxiously)* You see? That's all I put!

HARRIETTE. *All?*

PETER. But, good Lord, Uncle, do you realize what you've done—er—rather what you've left undone?

HUMPHREY. What?

PETER. You haven't even *suggested* marriage! All you've done is offer her the choice of a double or single bed!

(HARRIETTE wails)

HUMPHREY *(aghast)* What? But I *meant* marriage.

PETER. But you haven't *said so* here. *(Reading)* 'Bachelor clergyman would like to meet lady who would love, cherish and cook'—not a word about marriage—only the choice of a double or single bed!

HARRIETTE. Arthur, I think I am going to kill you!

PETER. No wonder the Press are on to this! No wonder they want your photograph!

HARRIETTE *(to Humphrey)* You've made yoursef a laughing stock all over the country!

HUMPHREY *(wailing)* No—no!

HARRIETTE *(rising)* And what will happen if the Church authorities get to hear about this? You'll be dismissed from the parish; possibly unfrocked—excommunicated ...

PETER. Burnt at the stake!

HARRIETTE. Why did you do it? *Why? Why? Why?*

HUMPHREY *(babbling)* I had to do *something*, Harriette. You'd given Mrs Carter notice, and the thought of *your* cooking and—and 'Shreddi-wex' for the rest of my life ...!

HARRIETTE *(moving to the stairs)* I can't listen to any more! I think I shall go mad! I'm going to lie down; my head is spinning!

HUMPHREY. Shall I slip down to the village and get you some aspirin?

HARRIETTE. Don't you dare show your face in the village! What you *will* do is, get—(*pointing to the letters*) all these out of this room before I come down! Then go up to your bedroom and stay there—out of harm's way!

(HARRIETTE *exits upstairs*)

HUMPHREY (*moving above the letters*) But what can I *do* about the letters? It seems very impolite not to read them!

PETER. Look, Uncle, you can't read 'em all. (*Going to the letters*) You take this lot up to your room and ... and I'll go through the rest. (*He scoops up several letters and gives them to Humphrey*)

HUMPHREY (*going upstairs*) Oh, but my dear boy! I can't ask you to take all that trouble.

PETER. No trouble at all, Uncle! I'm going to have the time of my life!

HUMPHREY (*on the stairs*) Oh well! But, Peter ...

PETER. Yes, Uncle?

HUMPHREY. If you should come across one that seems—er—promising ... !

PETER. Promising! You mean one that prefers a *double* bed?

HUMPHREY (*absently*) Yes. (*Then horrified*) Oh!

(HUMPHREY *exits upstairs.* PETER *squats on his haunches by the letters, takes one up from the pile, and reads to himself*)

PETER (*reading the letter, then bursting out into laughter*) Hells bells! (*Reading to himself*) '—not an expert cook, but can offer more exciting qualifications!' (*He roars with laughter and rolls on his back*)

(A YOUNG MAN, *with a trilby hat shoved to the back of his head, appears at the french window*)

MAN (*taking in the situation quickly*) 'Scuse me, Vicar!

PETER (*still laughing*) Eh? (*He sits up*)

MAN (*quickly*) D'you mind?

PETER (*still not 'with it'*) Not at all—what?

MAN. Thanks a lot. (*Quickly producing a camera and raising it*) Hold it! (*He clicks the camera*)

PETER. *What?*

MAN (*cheerily*) Thanks, Vicar!

(*The* MAN *departs quickly*)

PETER (*leaping up*) What the ... ? (*Then in a terrific panic*) Hey, just a minute there! (*He dashes towards the window*) I'm not the Vicar! I'm ... (*Stopping at the window*) Oh—my—God!

CURTAIN

SCENE 2

SCENE—*The same. The next morning.*

When the CURTAIN *rises, the room is empty. By the window is a wheelbarrow with letters piled up on it. Several more piles of letters are on the desk and around it. The telephone is ringing, likewise the front door bell. After a moment or two,* MRS CARTER *rushes in from the kitchen looking very distrait.*

MRS CARTER (*to herself as she comes in*) For Gawd's sake . . . ! (*She hesitates* C *for a moment, wondering which bell to answer first, then rushes across to the phone. Picking up the phone and shouting down it*) No! (*She slams the receiver down, then moves* C *again*)

(*The front door bell is still ringing*)

(*Again to herself*) If that's another of them . . . ! (*She moves towards the hall* L)

(HARRIETTE, *also looking distrait, appears on the stairs. She is carrying a breakfast tray*)

HARRIETTE. Mrs Carter, if that is another of those reporters . . .
MRS CARTER. I'll give him hell!

(MRS CARTER *exits down* L. *The telephone rings*)

HARRIETTE (*wailing to herself*) Oh no! (*She comes quickly down the stairs, puts the tray on the table* C *and crosses to the phone. On her way she sees the barrow-load of letters and gives a louder wail*) Aaah! (*Charging at the phone she knocks a pile of letters off the desk accidentally. As they fall to the floor she gives another wail*) Aaah! (*She then speaks into the phone. There is an almost hysterical note in her voice throughout the conversation*) The Vic . . . (*quickly*) Stebbington-Fawley two-four-one . . . Who is speaking? . . . Oh no! . . . (*wildly*) I'm sorry! The Vicar is not at home! . . . No, I'm afraid not . . . Absolutely impossible! . . . No, no, it's out of the question . . . Please, you're wasting your time—and mine. I have already *told* you the Vicar . . . Who am *I*? I am his sister! . . . Would I *what*? . . . Most certainly *not*! Good morning! (*She slams down the receiver*) Oh! Oh! Oh! (*She runs her hand over her brow distractedly, then gets down on hands and knees, and begins to collect the fallen letters.*)

(*A door slams down* L, *and* MRS CARTER *enters*)

(*Seeing her*) Was it a reporter?
MRS CARTER (*grimly*) It was!
HARRIETTE. Did you . . . ?

Mrs Carter. I did! But not before 'e'd 'eard a few words I'll bet 'e'd never 'eard before—a few of Carter's.

Harriette (*horrified*) Mrs Carter, you didn't swear at him?

Mrs Carter. Well, I didn't sing him the twenty-third psalm!

Harriette. Much more of this and I shall end up in a madhouse!

Mrs Carter. Much more of it, and we *all* shall—and we shan't notice much difference. Shall I give you a hand with *them*? (*Indicating the letters*)

Harriette (*almost wildly*) No, no! Just leave me alone.

Mrs Carter. O.K. (*moving to the kitchen door*) I'll deal with the next lot!

(Harriette *gives a loud wail and continues picking up letters.* Mrs Carter *exits to the kitchen.* Humphrey *appears at the top of the stairs and begins to descend. He is wearing a silk scarf over his dog collar. He sees Harriette on the floor, gives a little 'Oh!' of alarm, turns and begins to creep stealthily back upstairs*)

Harriette (*turning in time to catch him*) Arthur!

Humphrey (*stopping*) Yes, Harriette?

Harriette (*waving her hand, indicating the letters*) Are these all this morning's?

Humphrey. 'Fraid so, my dear! (*He comes down to* L *of her*)

Harriette. You know where you can put them, don't you?

Humphrey (*after a slight pause*) All of them?

Harriette. All of them—straight on the bonfire.

Humphrey (*turning the letters over*) But there may be one or two *ordinary* one's amongst them.

Harriette. It can't be helped! They'll have to go too.

Humphrey (*picking up a buff-coloured envelope and looking at it*) Income tax! That can certainly go! (*He drops it back on the pile*)

(*Between them they put the letters in tidy piles during the following*)

(*Gingerly*) Er—was that the telephone I heard just now, Harriette?

Harriette. It *was*!

Humphrey (*still gingerly*) *Oh!* Anything to do with—er . . . ?

Harriette (*sharply*) Everything to do with it. It was the B.B.C. wanting to know if you would be interviewed this evening.

Humphrey. Goodness gracious! What did you tell them?

Harriette. I told them you would *not*.

Humphrey. Oh! Quite right—I suppose.

Harriette. You *suppose*?

Humphrey (*with a sigh*) I've always had a—a secret hope that one day I might be asked to appear on television. I have—er—certain theories which might be helpful to viewers.

HARRIETTE. And is sharing a double bed with the cook incorporated in one of them?

(PETER, *with a newspaper in his hand, comes down the stairs. He is still wearing the parson's collar*)

PETER (*timorously*) Morning, Auntie!

HARRIETTE (*picking up a paper from the desk and sitting in the armchair*) Don't you speak to me!

PETER. Oh! (*To Humphrey*) We're *both* in the dog-house, are we?

HUMPHREY. I'm afraid so, my boy.

PETER. Never mind! Actions speak louder than words! (*He looks at the paper he is carrying, then without a word slips it gingerly on to Harriette's lap. The paper is folded at a particular page with a photograph on it. He points to the photograph*) Wait for the explosion, Uncle. (*He puts a finger in each ear and closes his eyes*)

HUMPHREY. What? Is there going to be a bang? (*He also puts a finger in each ear*)

(HARRIETTE *looks down at the paper for a moment, then holds her paper, similarly folded, out to Peter*)

PETER (*after a moment*) No explosion? (*He opens his eyes and sees Harriette's paper under his nose*) But, Auntie, haven't you seen . . . ? (*He breaks off*) But this isn't my paper . . . (*Then as he looks at the paper again*) Oh my god—fathers! It's in here too!

HARRIETTE (*grimly*) It is! I don't suppose there's a paper it isn't in.

PETER. It'll be in the *War Cry* on Saturday! (*Appealingly*) Auntie—(*looking at the paper*)—tell me—and you don't have to be polite——

(HARRIETTE *glares at him*)

I mean you've enough on your plate without that, haven't you? But—the photograph—it isn't a *good* one of me, is it? I mean —if you didn't know it was me, you wouldn't've recognized me, would you?

HARRIETTE (*looking at him, not at the photograph*) You look like the village idiot!

PETER. You don't mean that normally I look like the village . . .

HARRIETTE. No. Normally you just behave like him.

PETER (*gratefully*) Bless you for those kind words. (*He moves* LC) Then you don't think anyone will recognize me as—er— 'Venture Man'?

HUMPHREY (*moving* R *of Peter*) It doesn't look like you a bit,

PETER. It doesn't look like me, either. Although it *says* it's me. I don't know what the villagers will think!

HARRIETTE. I shudder to think about their thoughts since that wretched advertisement appeared.

PETER. Well, Uncle, between us, we've certainly hit the headlines! What with my disappearance and your single beds!

(MRS CARTER *comes in from the kitchen*)

MRS CARTER (*still with eyes only for Peter*) 'Scuse me!

HARRIETTE. Yes? What is it, Mrs Carter?

MRS CARTER (*moving* L *of Harriette*) You said you wanted me to do the shopping this morning, instead of you.

(HUMPHREY *moves down* L)

HARRIETTE. Yes, I do—er—please. Er—thank you, Mrs Carter, you're very kind.

MRS CARTER (*noting the politeness*) Ooh! You are upset, aren't you? Well, I'd better have a list, 'adn't I? (*Gazing at Peter*) This last few days I 'aven't been able to think straight. Don't know whether I'm comin' or goin'. (*Giggling at Peter and giving him a nudge with her elbow*) Carter swears I'm *goin'*—up the pole!

HARRIETTE (*rising*) You're not the only one! (*Wailing*) I'm going *up* it!

HUMPHREY. Harriette!

HARRIETTE (*snapping at him*) And you've *never* been *down* it! Come into the kitchen, Mrs Carter. (*Moving to the kitchen*) I'll make out a list.

(HARRIETTE *exits into the kitchen.* MRS CARTER *starts to follow*)

PETER. Mrs Carter . . .

MRS CARTER (*returning like a shot from a gun*) Yes, my lovely?

PETER. You still haven't told your husband—about me being here, I mean?

MRS CARTER. If I 'ad, you wouldn't *be* here!

PETER. What?

MRS CARTER. 'E'd've been up here with 'is rabbiting gun, and you'd've 'ad it!

PETER. Oh my God!

MRS CARTER. Ooh! 'ates the sight of you, Carter does! The times I've 'ad to stop him putting 'is boot through the telly when you've been on!

PETER. A critic, is he?

MRS CARTER. Jealous—that's his trouble. He knows you're my 'eart-throb, and he says if my heart's goin' to throb for anybody, it ought to throb for him.

HUMPHREY. Well, of course—those who have been joined together in Holy Wedlock . . .

MRS CARTER (*not really sharply*) The less *you* say about 'Holy Wedlock' the better!

HUMPHREY. Oh!

PETER (*quickly*) Ahem! Well, I hope I never meet your husband, Mrs Carter.

MRS CARTER. 'E's often said if ever he *did* meet you, it wouldn't be my 'eart that'd be throbbing but your bloody 'ead!

HUMPHREY. Mrs. Carter!

MRS CARTER. 'Is very words, Vicar, if I drop down dead!

(HARRIETTE'S *voice is heard off in the kitchen*)

HARRIETTE (*off*) Mrs Carter!

MRS CARTER (*calling*) Coming! (*To Peter*) Oh! (*With a tremor in the voice*) You're—you're beautiful!

(MRS CARTER *dashes off into the kitchen*)

HUMPHREY (*sighing*) How wonderful to command such—such adoration; such attention!

PETER. Well, I don't know about 'adoration', but you can't grumble at the amount of attention you're commanding just now, Uncle! What's the betting that you'll have the House Full boards out at church next Sunday?

HUMPHREY (*delighted*) You think so?

PETER. Might have to put on an extra matinee!

HUMPHREY (*crossing to the window*) I wonder if I dare go down to the potting shed?

PETER. What for, Uncle?

HUMPHREY. I usually work out my sermons down there. And if I'm to deliver three on Sunday . . . ! But Harriette said I wasn't to put my nose outside the house.

PETER. H'm! (*Moving R of Humphrey*) Bit awkward! You can't very well leave it behind.

HUMPHREY (*producing a pair of dark sunglasses*) Perhaps if I wore these. (*He puts them on*)

PETER. Marvellous. Nice glasses, Uncle; they suit you!

HUMPHREY (*pleased*) You think so?

PETER. Smashing! Much better than mine. Where did you get them?

HUMPHREY. Your dressing-table.

(HUMPHREY *exits into the garden*)

PETER. Well I'll be . . .

(MRS CARTER *enters from the kitchen*)

MRS CARTER. Anything you want while I'm in the village, my lovely?

PETER (*moving to her*) Yes. A pair of sunglasses.

MRS CARTER. Right. You shall 'ave 'em. A present from me! To remember me by. (*She moves close to him*)

PETER. In that case—you'd better get them rose-tinted. (*He puts his arm round her*)

MRS CARTER (*in ecstasy*) Gawd! (*Lying in Peter's arms*) If only the world could see me now—locked in the arms of 'Venture Man'!

(HARRIETTE *enters from the kitchen with a paper in her hand*)

HARRIETTE. *Mrs* Carter!

MRS CARTER (*breaking away from Peter*) My one big moment, and you 'ave to come an' sully it!

(MRS CARTER *exits into the kitchen*)

HARRIETTE (*moving down* c) How you can fool around at a time like this . . . ! (*Holding out the paper*) This is Mrs Carter's paper. Just read what it says about Arthur! He'll never live this down! Never! Oh! The shame! The humiliation! If the Bishop hears about this!

PETER. Uncle's Bishop?

HARRIETTE (*nodding*) Lax.

PETER. Lax? What's that short for? (*Quickly*) No, don't tell me!

HARRIETTE. The Bishop of Lax! He'll be appalled—livid!

PETER. Waxy Lax!

(*The telephone rings*)

HARRIETTE (*wildly*) That phone again! I can't answer it! I can't! It's bound to be a reporter, or the B.B.C., or one of those ghastly women!

PETER. Look, Auntie, let me deal with it. Why don't you go upstairs?

HARRIETTE (*almost hysterically*) I've only just come *down* stairs! I've spent practically the last two days upstairs! I can't stay upstairs for ever!

PETER. What a pity!

(*The telephone is still ringing*)

HARRIETTE. And what's the use of going upstairs? (*Wailing loudly*) How can I sleep, what with thinking about Arthur, and that—(*she is getting hysterical*) that *bloody* phone . . . !

PETER. *Auntie!*

HARRIETTE. I'm going mad! I'm going mad! I must be!

PETER. Not half you aren't! Now look, Auntie . . . (*To the phone*) Oh shut up! (*To himself*) My God! I am too! (*To Harriette*) Auntie, in my room, in the chest of drawers, third

drawer down, there's a bottle of whisky. Why don't you just
have a little nip of it? It'll do you a world of good.
HARRIETTE (*still hysterically*) Certainly not! I never drink!
Not even my own dandelion wine.
PETER. Well, that's understandable! But I'm sure just the
teeniest drop of whisky would settle your nerves.
HARRIETTE (*moving to the stairs with wild gesture*) No! No!
I wouldn't think of it! I would rather die a thousand times!
(*Mounting the stairs*) Ten thousand times! Twenty! (*Turning
at the top of the stairs; whimpering*) Did you say the *third*
drawer down?

(HARRIETTE *exits upstairs, whimpering.* PETER, *grinning,
goes to the telephone*)

PETER (*very loudly and curtly*) Hello! . . . No, you can't! . . .
Never mind whether he's at home or not, he's not available . . .

(*While Peter is speaking on the phone,* JOSEPHINE DE
BRISSAC *appears at the french window.* JOSEPHINE *is definitely
'mutton dressed as lamb'. She wears an old-fashioned large-
flowered voile dress, with bits hanging from it at several
points; much cheap jewellery, her hair is dyed bright yellow;
her hat is large, floppy, and adorned with flowers, fruit and
ribbons. Amongst other impedimenta, she carries a cardboard
cakebox.* JOSEPHINE *is decidedly an eccentric. Seeing Peter at
the desk, she trips lightly and gaily into the room, and down
towards him. When just behind him, she pulls up, realizing
he is 'on the phone'; she puts a hand to her mouth, as if to
stop herself speaking, then, looking around the room she
begins to twirl girlishly round it, arms 'undulating'. During
her twirls she puts the cakebox on the table up* C. *She takes
no notice of Peter's conversation*)

PETER (*unaware of Josephine's entrance; into the phone
during all the above*) . . . You've got to speak to him? Don't make
me laugh, brother! . . . Do I know who you are? . . . I don't care
who the hell you are . . . (*With a yelp*) What did you say? You
are the Bishop of Lax! . . . (*He makes almost hysterical, and
completely unintelligible noises as he fumblingly replaces the
receiver on the hook. He backs away from the desk with hands
in front of him as if the phone were following him*) The Bishop
of . . . ! The Bishop of . . . ! The Bishop . . .

(PETER *backs* LC *and bumps into Josephine*)

JOSEPHINE (*ecstatically; shrill*) Aaaah!
PETER (*panic-stricken*) Aaah! (*He turns and sees Josephine*)
Oh my . . . !

(JOSEPHINE *sways in ecstasy.* PETER, *forgetting he is dis-*

guised, imagines it is the usual 'faint'. Automatically his hands go out. JOSEPHINE, *with a whinny of delight, flies into them*)

JOSEPHINE. Beloved! (*Her arms go round him*)

PETER. Blind O'Reilly!

JOSEPHINE. No, no! Don't speak! Don't speak! 'We need no words, we two. Our thoughts are one!'

PETER. They're not, y'know; at least I hope not!

JOSEPHINE (*gazing at him adoringly*) Ar-thur!

PETER. Eh?

JOSEPHINE (*with emotion*) Arthur!

PETER. Now look . . . ! (*He tries to get away from her*)

JOSEPHINE (*intensely*) I am looking, beloved. Looking back over the endless years that have divided us—and thanking *The Times* for bringing us together again!

PETER. Bringing us . . . ? I've never seen you before in my life! (*He moves back*)

JOSEPHINE (*moving to him*) Not in this life, beloved! But— think back, Arthur! Think back! Back through time to that day you first saw me from your chariot!

PETER (*gaping*) My . . . ?

JOSEPHINE (*sweeping on*) Ah! Now you remember (*Putting her arms round him*) The mists of time are rolling by!

PETER (*struggling*) Now listen—er—girlie . . .

JOSEPHINE (*coyly*) Josephine.

PETER (*breaking away* R) You must be . . . (*He was going to say 'nuts'*)

JOSEPHINE (*following him; delighted*) I am! I am! I am that very she whom you saw on the dusty highway—so very long ago. Remember? You drew your horses to a halt . . .

PETER (*yelping*) Horses?

JOSEPHINE. You pulled me to your side, and together we rode out into the sunset; the lowly slave and the mighty Emperor! (*She falls on her knees, her arms round his legs*)

PETER. Are you sure you're not confusing me with Ben Hur?

JOSEPHINE (*gesturing wildly with one arm*)
        'Or ever the knightly years were gone,
          With the old world to the grave,
        You were a King in Babylon
        And *I* was a Christian slave.'

(*She rises and twirls away* L) Why didn't you answer my letter, Arthur?

PETER. Your . . . ? I'd run out of parchment!

JOSEPHINE (*lying on the settee and beckoning to him*) The moment I saw your 'heart-cry' in *The Times*, I knew, I *knew* you were calling to me again! I took pen in hand and wrote to you at once. And then I waited—and waited—oh, how I waited!

PETER (*muttering*) And, oh! how you'll wait!

JOSEPHINE (*springing to her feet*) But I could wait no longer! The call was too strong! I had to come to you (*Opening her arms wide*) And here I am.

PETER. Not half you aren't!

JOSEPHINE. Beloved! (*She rushes at Peter again*)

(PETER *puts out an arm to ward her off, but* JOSEPHINE *evades it, skilfully, and then leans well back on Peter's arm silent-film 'vamp-wise'. She ogles him from this position for a moment or two*)

PETER (*extending his free arm*) What is your problem?

(*Swiftly* JOSEPHINE *spins round and leans even further back on Peter's other arm*)

Stand up straight, woman! I'll let you go with such a bump in a minute!

JOSEPHINE (*stroking his face, still leaning back*) Master!

(HUMPHREY, *without sunglasses or scarf, comes running in from the french windows, carrying a letter, without an envelope*)

HUMPHREY (*as he enters*) Peter! Peter!

PETER (*wildly*) Uncle! Uncle! Help!

HUMPHREY (*intent on the letter, coming to* L *of Peter*) Peter! I've found someone!

PETER. So have I!

HUMPHREY. What? (*Seeing Josephine on Peter's arm—vaguely*) Oh, good morning! (*Then quickly to Peter*) Peter, this letter! It's from a lady near London. She says she is around thirty—adores the country—yearns for someone to love and cherish——

PETER (*struggling desperately with Josephine*) Uncle, do shut up a minute. I mean—one thing at a time!

HUMPHREY (*still with the letter*) —she can cook! And she swears——

PETER. That'll be a help!

HUMPHREY. —swears that we have met before in the— (*referring to the letter*) 'in the distant past'.

JOSEPHINE (*straightening up*) What?

HUMPHREY. I can't call her to mind at the moment!

JOSEPHINE. My letter!

HUMPHREY (*blinking*) I beg your . . . ?

JOSEPHINE (*snatching the letter from him*) Yes! My letter—to Arthur!

HUMPHREY. Peter—who is this?

JOSEPHINE. 'Peter'! (*To Peter*) Do you mean that you are not—not Arthur?

PETER. No, I'm not! And aren't I lucky?

JOSEPHINE. Then—then—(*turning to Humphrey*) you—*you* are Arthur?

HUMPHREY. Well—er—yes! (*He backs away a little*)

JOSEPHINE (*advancing a step*) Of course! Of course! I realize that now! How could I have made such a mistake?

HUMPHREY (*holding out his arms—to protect himself*) Madam —I . . .

JOSEPHINE (*flying into his arms*) Aaaah!

HUMPHREY (*in panic*) Aaah! Peter!

PETER (*dashing towards the french window*) 'Scuse me, Uncle! I've got to see several men about several dogs!

(PETER *exits through the french windows.* HUMPHREY *moves* C. JOSEPHINE *follows and puts her arms round him*)

HUMPHREY (*babbling*) Madam!

JOSEPHINE. Beloved! (*She holds him firmly*)

HUMPHREY. This is most . . . !

JOSEPHINE. No! no! Don't speak! 'We need no words, we two. Our thoughts are one!'

HUMPHREY. But I'm not thinking. I'm scarcely breathing! (*He gasps for breath*)

JOSEPHINE. Arthur!

HUMPHREY (*feebly trying to get away*) Madam, look, if you would only . . .

JOSEPHINE (*intensely*) I *am* looking, beloved! Looking back over the endless years that have divided us—and thanking *The Times* for bringing us together again!

HUMPHREY. Are you *quite* sure we've met before? I hardly think I should have forgotten.

JOSEPHINE. Think back, Arthur! Think back! Back through time to the day you first saw me from your chariot!

HUMPHREY (*puzzled*) You mean the old Morris-Cowley? But that was way back in . . .

JOSEPHINE. Go further back, beloved!

HUMPHREY (*struggling feebly*) I'm trying to. (*He backs a step with Josephine still clinging to him*) Before the Morris-Cowley I had a bicycle . . .

JOSEPHINE. Back! Back! Let the mists of time roll by!

HUMPHREY (*desperately*) Madam, I am beginning to think you must be . . .

JOSEPHINE. I *am*! I *am*! I am that very she whom you saw on the dusty highway—so very long ago. Remember? You drew your horses to a halt . . .

HUMPHREY. But—I've never driven *one* horse, let alone *two*!

JOSEPHINE (*kneeling with her arms round Humphrey's legs*) You pulled me to your side, and together we rode out into the sunset; the lowly slave and the mighty Emperor!

HUMPHREY. You have the most amazing memory!
JOSEPHINE. 'Or ever the knightly years were gone,
With the old world to the grave,
You were a King in Babylon,
And *I* was a Christian slave.'

(HUMPHREY *breaks free*)

HUMPHREY (*feeling an aching arm and moving away*) Oh!
That's better! (*Then turning to Josephine*) Well now . . . !
JOSEPHINE (*bounding across the room*) Beloved!
HUMPHREY (*seeing her coming*) Oh, not again! (*An arm goes out*)

(JOSEPHINE *is on to the arm like a shot, leaning back and ogling Humphrey*)

(*Suddenly pulling himself free*) Madam, please—I must insist!
Before we can begin to think of—er—loving and cherishing
there is quite a lot to be done. (*Moving away from her a little, then turning to face her*) Now first of all, I must take down your particulars.
JOSEPHINE (*after a slight pause*) Here—and now?
HUMPHREY. Here—and now! (*Moving to the desk and sitting*) You must remember I have had several replies to my advertisement . . .
JOSEPHINE. Oh! I see what you mean!
HUMPHREY (*taking pen and paper*) And I must—in fairness give them all some consideration!
JOSEPHINE. But—Arthur . . . !
HUMPHREY. Now—er—what was the name again? My memory . . . ! (*Very businesslike*) Surname?
JOSEPHINE (*twirling* LC) De Brissac. But Arthur—beloved . . . !
HUMPHREY (*writing*) De Brissac! Ah! French?
JOSEPHINE. On my mother's side. (*She lies on the settee*)
HUMPHREY. And on your father's?
JOSEPHINE. Mother didn't get time to ask him.
HUMPHREY (*writing*) You are from Paris?
JOSEPHINE. Putney. (*She turns over on her stomach*)
HUMPHREY (*writing*) Put-ney. Er—Christian name?
JOSEPHINE. Josephine.
HUMPHREY (*writing*) Josephine.
JOSEPHINE. The Empress Josephine—I was christened after her.
HUMPHREY (*turning and looking at her*) Roughly—how *long* after?
JOSEPHINE. Beloved, it is all in the letter.
HUMPHREY. Er—quite! I think you said your age was 'around thirty'?

JOSEPHINE (*waving her arms, dismissing the subject*) Yes, yes! Around thirty.

HUMPHREY (*after a doubtful look at her; politely*) Er—within what radius?

JOSEPHINE. In wisdom—I am a thousand years old!

HUMPHREY (*writing; amiably*) That's about what I thought! (*Slight pause*) Now—what next? Oh yes! Er—'love and cherish, and ... (*Quickly*) But we can leave the 'love and cherish'. You've already demonstrated fully—er ... ! 'Cooking'! Most important!

JOSEPHINE (*rushing and picking up the cakebox*) My speciality!

HUMPHREY (*rising and moving to her side*) What ... er ... ?

JOSEPHINE (*opening the box and showing him the contents*) Fairy cakes!

HUMPHREY (*amiably*) Oh! Fairy ... !

JOSEPHINE. Take one, beloved! I made them for you!

HUMPHREY. Oh—er—thank you! (*He takes a small cake from the box, and looks at it. Happily*) Fairy cakes! (*He takes a small bite from the cake*)

JOSEPHINE (*after a slight pause; anxiously*) Yes?

HUMPHREY (*guardedly*) Oh yes, yes indeed! (*Moving to the desk, sitting and writing*) Speciality—rock buns. (*He drops the cake into his tin wastepaper-basket, where—being in reality a painted stone—it lands with a loud clang*)

JOSEPHINE (*twirling round the room*) How happy I shall be, Arthur in my little kitchen, cooking for you! Wonderful dishes —with spices from the Orient--full of Eastern promise!

HUMPHREY. I rather favour western *nourishment*. However ... (*Rising*) Thank you very much for calling Miss de Brissac. It is *Miss* de Brissac, I presume?

JOSEPHINE (*twirling*) More or less!

HUMPHREY (*blinking*) More or ... ?

JOSEPHINE (*running to him and grabbing his hand*) Now, shall we go down to the bus station together, and collect my things?

HUMPHREY. Your ... ! But ... !

JOSEPHINE. I haven't brought—everything; just the essentials —(*coyly; lowering her eyes*) for the night.

HUMPHREY (*with a yelp*) The night! Did you say the *night*?

JOSEPHINE (*putting her arms around him*) Are you afraid, beloved?

HUMPHREY. Afraid? I'm petrified!

JOSEPHINE. Afraid you will wake in the morning and find me gone!

HUMPHREY (*babbling*) But I have no intention of waking in the morning and finding you *there*!

JOSEPHINE (*purring*) 'Josephine' ...

HUMPHREY. Josephine—er—that is—oh my goodness!

JOSEPHINE. Tonight, beloved, we will recapture that *other*

night—so long ago—when we lay together on the hot desert sands. Remember?

HUMPHREY (*babbling*) I'm sure you must be mistaken. The nearest I've ever been to the hot sands was a matinee of *The Desert Song*!

JOSEPHINE (*spinning round on to his other arm and bending back*) Tonight, Arthur—tonight!

HUMPHREY (*firmly*) Not tonight, Josephine!

JOSEPHINE. *Tonight!* (*She flings her arms around him*)

(*There is a ring at the front door bell*)

HUMPHREY. There's someone at the door! Thank goodness! (*Muttering*) Heaven is very merciful!

(JOSEPHINE *releases him*)

Now—(*fluttering around*) if you wouldn't mind leaving by the window. It might save awkward explanations.

JOSEPHINE. Arthur—you're not sending me away? Where shall I go?

HUMPHREY. Er—whence you came! You did get a return ticket?

(*The door bell rings again*)

JOSEPHINE. But Arthur . . .

HUMPHREY (*dashing around picking up Josephine's bag and cakebox*) These are yours, are they not? Now—you will be hearing from me when the mists of time roll by. In the meantime—shall we say 'Good-bye'?

JOSEPHINE. 'Good-bye'? You mean 'Au revoir'!

HUMPHREY. Do I? Fancy me thinking I didn't!

(*The door bell rings again*)

Oh dear! (*He shepherds Josephine towards the window*) Now—you can let yourself out? I must answer that bell.

JOSEPHINE. Arthur—beloved . . . ! (*She is about to fling herself into his arms*)

(*But* HUMPHREY *is prepared for it. He dodges her embrace neatly*)

HUMPHREY. Er—*do* notice the petunias as you go. They're coming along nicely this year! (*Moving quickly to the arch* L) Goodbye! (*Waving, with his back to Josephine*) Good-bye!

(HUMPHREY *exits down* L. *As soon as he has gone,* JOSEPHINE *darts across to the arch and peeps cautiously through it*)

PIXIE (*off*) Where is he? Where is he?

JOSEPHINE (*furious*) Oh! A rival! (*She looks around for somewhere to hide—then crosses quickly to the screen and gets behind it*)

(PIXIE (*I'll Get My Man*) POTTER *comes quickly in* L, *followed by a flustered* HUMPHREY. PIXIE *is a 'very much with it' girl of twenty, and wears typical 'with it' attire*)

PIXIE (*as she enters*) I gotta see him, I tell you. I gotta! (*She moves* C)

HUMPHREY (*flustered*) But, my dear young lady . . . (*Moving* L *of her; puzzled*) You *are* a girl, aren't you?

PIXIE. *What?*

HUMPHREY. One can never be absolutely certain these days!

PIXIE. Whadja think I am? A gorilla?

HUMPHREY. Good gracious, no! A gorilla has bigger teeth!

PIXIE. You talk as if you don't know who I am!

HUMPHREY (*blinking*) Er—should I know you? (*Then with a yelp of alarm*) Oh no! Don't tell me you're another!

PIXIE. Another what?

HUMPHREY. Don't tell me I once laid with *you* on the hot desert sands!

PIXIE (*gaping at him*) You dirty old man!

HUMPHREY. Really! I resent that! You called me 'old'!

PIXIE (*striding around*) Oh, belt up! You're wasting my time. Get weavin'; find the Vicar of this dump and tell him Pixie Potter wants to see him.

HUMPHREY (*floundering*) Pixie—er—*what* name?

PIXIE. For Pete's sake, you're not going to tell me you've never even *heard* of Pixie ('I'll Get My Man') Potter?

HUMPHREY. Oh, yes indeed; I've heard of you. You are a well-known soprano.

PIXIE. Sopra——? What's that for God's sake?

HUMPHREY (*gaping at her*) Well, you—er—*sing*, don't you?

PIXIE. You accusin' me of bein' old-fashioned?

HUMPHREY. What?

PIXIE. Aw, cut it, grand-dad, will you, an' go and get this Vicar guy.

HUMPHREY. But I am the Vicar guy—er . . . !

PIXIE (*gaping at him*) *You?*

HUMPHREY. *Me.* I!

PIXIE (*with derision*) Yeah?

HUMPHREY (*with certainty*) Yeah! Er—yes!

(PIXIE *promptly takes a folded newspaper from her coat pocket, looks at the photograph on it, then looks at Humphrey*)

PIXIE. Well, if this—(*referring to the photograph*) is you—then I'm Lonnie Donegan.

HUMPHREY. I'm afraid the comparison is lost on me; I don't know Miss Donegan.

PIXIE (*staring at him*) You ain't real—you ain't, honest! You'll

be tellin' me next you've never heard of Peter ('Venture Man')
Graham!

HUMPHREY. Peter . . . (*Flustered*) Oh yes, I've—I've heard of
him!

PIXIE (*with mock surprise*) You *have*? My! My!

HUMPHREY. Well, considering he's my . . . (*He pulls up
quickly*)

PIXIE (*sharply*) Your *what*?

HUMPHREY (*moving away; terribly embarrassed*) My—er—my
er . . .

PIXIE (*after a look at him; almost to herself*) Jeez! P'raps you're
talking sense! P'raps you *are* the Vic . . . !

HUMPHREY (*still babbling*) My—er—my—er . . .

PIXIE (*looking at the paper*) And p'raps he *isn't* . . . (*To
Humphrey*) Hey!

HUMPHREY. I beg your pardon?

PIXIE (*holding out the paper*) This photograph! See what it
says under it?

HUMPHREY. It says—it says . . .

PIXIE. It says 'The Reverend Arthur Humphrey in his charming country Vicarage.' And you say *you* are this Humphrey guy?

HUMPHREY (*embarrassed*) Er—quite—quite!

PIXIE. But this isn't *you*?

HUMPHREY (*looking*) I don't photograph very well, but I
recognize the collar.

PIXIE. You're trying to pull a fast one on me, aren't you?

HUMPHREY (*moving towards the window*) Er—would you like
to come along and see . . .

PIXIE (*rushing to him, grabbing him and turning him around*)
You know who this—(*indicating the photograph*) is, don't you?

HUMPHREY. I—I—won't you come along and see the—the
petunias?

PIXIE. No, I won't! I saw 'em last week on the telly, and they
stink! (*Desperately; almost shouting*) Look! I gotta see—(*holding out the paper*) him! I gotta!

(*The front door bell rings*)

HUMPHREY. But I'm afraid . . .

PIXIE. I don't know what he's up to. P'raps he's in some sorta
trouble—so I can't say much, see? All I know is—(*brokenly*)
I gotta see him! I gotta!

HUMPHREY (*touched*) My dear young lady . . . (*He moves
towards her*)

PIXIE (*sobbing*) I gotta get my man! (*She lies on the settee on
her stomach, kicking her legs*)

HUMPHREY (*sitting gingerly beside her*) Now, now! Smack
botties!

(PETER *enters quickly through the french windows*)

c

PETER (*as he enters*) There's someone at the front door . . . (*He sees Pixie on the settee with Humphrey. In great alarm*) Aaah! (*He looks round very quickly then dives behind the screen. When behind it, he gives a louder yell*) Aaah!

PIXIE (*looking up; wildly*) That was him! That was his voice! I heard him! (*She runs about the room*)

(*The door bell rings again.* MRS CARTER *enters from the kitchen*)

MRS CARTER. There's someone at the front . . . (*Seeing Pixie*) 'Er! My Gawd! 'Er!

(*The door bell rings again*)

PIXIE. I heard him, I tell you! He's *here*! In this room! (*She suddenly darts to the screen, and pulls it aside*)

(PETER *is revealed standing with a bewildered* JOSEPHINE *bent well back in his arms*)

(*in horror*) Oh!

MRS CARTER (*also horrified*) Oh! My lovely!

PETER (*almost gibbering to Josephine*) Josephine, Josephine, beloved, think back, think back. Let the mists of time roll by! Think back over the endless years that have divided us . . .

(*Several things happen at once. The* BISHOP OF LAX *appears at the arch down* L *and stands just inside it. He is a very dignified man of sixty, in bishop's garb, and wearing his top hat*)

PIXIE (*almost at the same time; her eyes on Peter and Josephine*) Ooooh! (*Blindly she rushes to Humphrey on the settee and flings herself on him, sobbing*)

MRS CARTER (*almost at the same time; heartbroken*) Ooooh!

(*The* BISHOP *can only stand aghast*)

PETER (*meanwhile, without a pause*) —back through time to that day I first saw you from my chariot——

(HARRIETTE'S *voice is now heard singing from upstairs. She sings, from 'My Fair Lady', in a quavering voice but fairly quickly*)

HARRIETTE (*off*) 'I'm getting married in the morning!
          Ding-dong the bells are going to chime!'

(HARRIETTE *appears at the top of the stairs with an empty glass in her hand. She is very slightly tipsy, and happy. The* BISHOP *moves to the stairs, gaping at her*)

(*Standing at the top of the stairs; still singing*)
          'Pull out the stopper!
          Pour out a whopper!'

(Gently pirouetting on the landing)
            'But get me to the church on time!'

PETER *(declaiming through the song)* —I am that very he whom you saw on the dusty highway—so very long ago. Remember?

(The BISHOP *moves down* c)

I drew my horses to a halt, pulled you to my side, and together we rode out into the sunset; the lowly slave and the mighty Emperor! *(After Harriette has finished her song; almost bawling, with a sweeping gesture of his free arm, Josephine bent well back over the other)*

            'I was a King of Babylon,
            And you were a Christian slave!'

    MRS CARTER *flings herself sobbing into the Bishop's arms, as—*

            the CURTAIN *falls*

SCENE—*The same. The action is continuous.*

When the CURTAIN *rises,* JOSEPHINE *is still in* PETER'S *arms;* PIXIE *in* HUMPHREY'S, *and* MRS CARTER *in the* BISHOP'S. HARRIETTE *is at the top of the stairs. The kitchen door is open.*

BISHOP (*loudly*) May I ask . . . ?

(*The front door bell rings.* HARRIETTE *darts off along the corridor*)

(*Louder*) May I ask . . . ?

PETER (*suddenly, wildly and desperately*) Most certainly, sir! And your request is granted! (*Generally*) Ladies and gentlemen, at the request of our friend on the extreme left—will you now take your partners for—*The Merry Widow* waltz!

(PETER *immediately begins* 'La, la-ing' 'The Merry Widow', *pulls* JOSEPHINE *up into a dancing position and begins to waltz her clear of the screen then towards the french window*)

BISHOP. *What . . . ?*

PETER (*as they reach the window; to the bewildered* JOSEPHINE) Do you reverse? (*They reverse and waltz off through the window*)

(PETER *and* JOSEPHINE *exit through the french window. The door bell rings*)

HUMPHREY (*seeing Peter and Josephine go; panic-stricken*) No, no, don't go—don't leave me! Oh my . . . ! (*Quickly he begins to 'la-la' 'The Merry Widow' and waltzes Pixie to the kitchen door*)

(HUMPHREY *and* PIXIE *exit to the kitchen*)

BISHOP (*gaping*) What . . . ? (*Then aware of Mrs Carter in his arms*) My good woman!

MRS CARTER (*raising her head; brokenly*) All right, if you want to, though I don't feel like it! (*She begins to 'la-la' 'The Merry Widow' brokenly and waltzes the Bishop up* LC)

BISHOP (*babbling*) Madam—I beg you—this is dreadful!

MRS CARTER (*stopping dancing, moving away, hardly looking at the Bishop*) Well, I told you I didn't feel like it!

(MRS CARTER *bursts into sobs and exits to the kitchen. The door bell rings*)

BISHOP (*calling after Mrs Carter*) Come back! Come . . . (*He*

takes off his hat, puts it on the table up C, *and moves* RC, *panting)*
Outrageous! Outrageous! *(He wipes his brow with his handkerchief and collapses into the armchair)*

(A MAN'S VOICE *is heard off down* L)

VOICE *(off; irritably)* Oi! Anyone at 'ome?
BISHOP *(to himself)* Perfectly—outrageous!
VOICE *(off)* Oi !You!

(The BISHOP *sits up with a start)*

(off) Yus, you in the armchair; you deaf?
BISHOP *(looking off down* L *from the chair)* My good man . . . !
VOICE. Three times I rung this ruddy bell. D'y'want these ruddy letters or don't you?
BISHOP *(rising; angrily)* My good man! *(He moves* L)
VOICE. Wevver you do or you don't, I want my ruddy mailbag, so—get a move on, mate!
BISHOP *(as he goes)* Well really!

(The BISHOP *exits down* L. *After a moment he returns panting, with a mailbag clasped in his arms and moves to the desk. He stands for a moment, uncertain what to do with it.* MRS CARTER, *sniffing, enters quickly from the kitchen)*

MRS CARTER *(seeing the Bishop with the bag)* That's right. Just empty 'em on the floor—anywhere.

(MRS CARTER, dabbing her eyes with a handkerchief, goes quickly upstairs. The BISHOP *blinks after her for a moment, then up-ends the bag by the desk. A shoal of letters falls to the floor)*

BISHOP *(gaping at letters; staggered)* Good heavens! Incredible! *(He picks a letter up, looks at it, then sniffs it)* Pah!
VOICE *(off down* L) Oi! Mate! Don't go to sleep over the ruddy job!
BISHOP *(fuming)* I—I . . . ! Oh!

(The BISHOP *drops the letter in the pile and stamps off down* L *with the mailbag)*

VOICE *(off)* Ta, mate! Reckon *I* could do with a flunkey's job —just sittin' about in armchairs!

(A door is heard to slam. The BISHOP *enters* L)

BISHOP *(to himself)* Flunkey! *(He looks down at his gaitered legs)* 'T! 't! 't!

(MRS CARTER, still sniffing, appears on the landing. She sees the letters)

MRS CARTER *(with irritation)* Oh, look where you've . . . :

(*Coming down the stairs*) I know I said 'anywhere', but I didn't mean—*anywhere*. (*She goes down on her knees and begins piling them together in bundles*) You men, honest, you haven't the brains you were born with!

BISHOP. I—I ... (*He mops his brow with his handkerchief*)

MRS CARTER (*sniffing*) There ought to be a law against you—the whole lot of you! And there would be if I had my way!

BISHOP. Madam ...

MRS CARTER. Feckless, faithless creatures that you are!

BISHOP (*panicking a little*) Please ... please don't distress yourself ! I'll ... (*He gets on his knees L of her and begins piling the letters*)

MRS CARTER. I'm not distressing *myself*; it's been done for me. (*She snatches the Bishop's handkerchief and blows into it*)

BISHOP. But who has ... ?

MRS CARTER. The less said the better. Talkin' won't mend a broken heart, will it?

BISHOP. A broken ... ?

MRS CARTER. Well, punctured, anyway. (*She hands the Bishop his handkerchief*)

BISHOP (*soothingly*) Come, come, come, come!

MRS CARTER. It's no use you 'Come-come-come-ing'! You 'aven't had red-hot needles stuck in your heart, pulled out, and stuck in again, have you?

BISHOP. Frankly—no!

MRS CARTER. Ah! (*She dabs her eyes*) *He* did it to me—'my lovely'!

BISHOP. Er—your husband?

MRS CARTER (*with scorn*) What, Carter? Don't make me laugh!

BISHOP. Er—such was not my intention!

MRS CARTER. My heart-throb—it was him.

BISHOP. Your ... ? Are you telling me that there is another man in your life?

MRS CARTER I'm not telling you anything! My mother always used to say: 'Mollie, don't tell a man anything; leave him guessing!' (*Slight pause*) Poor old dad! He never did find out!

BISHOP (*rising; shocked*) Will you kindly tell the Vicar I am waiting to see him?

MRS CARTER (*sharply*) 'Ere! You're not another of them reporters, are you?

BISHOP (*indignantly*) Reporters?

MRS CARTER. Yes—disguised as (*with a wave towards his attire*) something or other?

BISHOP (*rising; angrily*) Really!

MRS CARTER (*rising*) I only asked! Well, I'll go and see what the Vicar says, but don't count your chickens. Oh, and you might finish gettin' that lot (*the letters*) straight while you're waiting; it'll help pass the time.

(*The telephone rings*)

(*Moving to the kitchen*) Oh, and you might answer that, wili you?

BISHOP (*moving* C; *fuming*) Will you kindly stop . . . !

MRS CARTER (*overlapping*) And when you do, don't say *nothing; nothing* at all! Ooh! You've no idea what's going on in here! (*Pointing to the kitchen door*)

(MRS CARTER *exits to the kitchen. The telephone continues to ring*)

BISHOP (*fuming*) Oh! (*He crosses to the phone, lifts the receiver, listens, shakes his head, listens, nods his head, listens, very firmly shakes his head, then replaces the receiver. He moves away from the desk a little, then stops, does a double-take as he realizes he never spoke on the phone. He puts his hand to his head, moves to the letters, and looks at them. To himself*) No, I'm damned if I—(*he looks round quickly*) blessed if I do!

(PIXIE'S *voice is heard in the kitchen*) *Off.*

PIXIE (*off; shouting*) I don't want another cup of coffee! All I want's—my man!   *ON*

(*The* BISHOP *quickly hides behind the armchair.* PIXIE *bursts into the room, followed by* HUMPHREY)

(*As she enters*) I've come here to get him—and I don't leave till I do! (*She moves to the armchair and throws herself into it*)

HUMPHREY (*moving* L *of the armchair; babbling*) But, my dear young lady . . .

PIXIE (*brokenly*) I love him, I tell you. Don't you know what love is?

HUMPHREY. I'm learning!

PIXIE. From the first moment I saw him. I loved that big slob! But he—he don't love me! He just looks at me as—as if I was poison! (*She begins to sob*)

HUMPHREY. Please—please don't cry! Have another cup of coffee instead!

PIXIE (*loudly*) Aw go and get . . .

HUMPHREY. Bovril?

PIXIE (*with a howl*) I want my man! (*With fervour*) And I'll get him! I'll get him if I have to . . . (*She suddenly jumps up, moves down* C, *and begins to 'sing' in a very raucous voice—with phoney actions*)

(*During the song,* HARRIETTE *appears at the top of the stairs, her hand to her head. On seeing Pixie, she pulls herself together and stands as if about to burst with anger*)

PIXIE (*'singing'*) 'I'll get my man!
                    I'll get my man!
                    I'll get my man!
                    If anyone can!'

(*The* BISHOP'S *face appears over the top of the armchair.
He watches, horrified*)

(*Clapping her hands and stamping* L *and then* R *foot to empha-
size*)

              'I/know/just/what/I'm/facin'
              It's/me'll/do/the/chasin'
              But I'll get my man!
              I'll get my man!——'

(HARRIETTE *comes downstairs*)

(*belting it out*) 'Yeah! Yeah! Yeah! Yeah!
              I'LL GET MY MAN!'

(*Speaking; sobbing*) I'll get my man . . .

(*The* BISHOP'S *face disappears behind the armchair.* HAR-
RIETTE *takes Pixie by the scruff of the neck*)

HARRIETTE (*firmly*) What you'll get, young woman, is a bath!
HUMPHREY. Harriette!

(*Without further ado,* HARRIETTE *marches the utterly bewildered and non-resisting* PIXIE *up the stairs and off.* HUM-
PHREY *gapes after them. The* BISHOP *crawls on hands and
knees from behind the armchair.* HUMPHREY *unconsciously
backs near the Bishop and, with a little smile, faces front and
begins to 'sing', stamp and clap*)

(*Singing and stamping awkwardly*)
              'I know just what I'm facin'
              It's me'll do the chasin'.'

(*On the 'chasin'' he accidentally stamps on the Bishop's hand*)
BISHOP (*with a howl*) Aaaah! (*He waves his hand in the air
in agony*)
HUMPHREY (*startled*) What? (*He turns and sees the Bishop*)
Oh my . . . ! (*He runs up the stairs, half muttering, half singing*)
'I'll get my man!'

(HUMPHREY *exits along the landing. The* BISHOP *groans
and nurses his hand*)

BISHOP (*groaning*) I must go! I must go! (*He puts his hand
to the floor, about to rise*)

(JOSEPHINE *flutters in from the french window*)

JOSEPHINE (*as she enters, calling*) Beloved! Beloved! (*She moves c, then sees the Bishop on the floor. Rapturously*) Aaah! (*She runs and kneels by his side*)

(*The* BISHOP, *when Josephine is near him, fearing his hand is going to be trodden on again, raises it quickly with a yelp*)

BISHOP. Aaah!

JOSEPHINE (*after looking at the Bishop intently; recoiling and holding her arms and hands out protectively*) No! No! I never laid on the desert sands with you! (*She rises quickly and flutters off down* L)

BISHOP (*by now completely shattered*) I must go! I must go! (*Trying to rise; rambling*) 'I will arise and go now, and go to Inisfree . . .' (*Realizing he is rambling, he groans and puts his hand to his head; still on his knees*)

(MRS CARTER *enters from the kitchen*)

MRS CARTER (*brightly*) Well, 'ow're you doin'?

(*The* BISHOP *groans*)

(*Looking at the letters*) Gawd! You're a right 'go-slow', aren't you? (*She moves* C)

BISHOP (*almost wailing*) Please . . .! (*Getting to his feet; desperately*) Please—I beg you—is there somewhere—anywhere—I can sit quietly for a few minutes and pull myself together?

MRS CARTER. Why—have you come apart?

BISHOP (*brokenly*) Madam—I don't *want* to strike you . . . !

MRS CARTER (*sharply*) If you did I'd strike you back!

(*The* BISHOP *whinnies*)

(*Softer*) There's a seat out in the garden—under the weeping willow.

BISHOP (*staggering to the french window*) Thank you.

MRS CARTER (*brightly*) Or if you'd rather come to bed . . . ?

BISHOP (*gaping at her in horror*) Oh!

(*The* BISHOP *staggers out of the window*)

MRS CARTER (*to herself*) Cor! You do meet 'em don't you? (*She begins putting the letters on the desk*)

(*After a moment,* PETER *peeps cautiously into the room from the window*)

PETER (*seeing Mrs Carter*) Psssst! Pssst!

MRS CARTER (*after looking at him coldly*) If you're 'Pssst-pssst'-ing at me, you can go and 'Pssst-pssst' somewhere else! I'm finished with *you*!

PETER (*coming near her; persuasively*) Mrs Carter . . .

MRS CARTER (*still putting letters on the desk or under it*) And it's no use 'Mrs Carter'-in'!

PETER. Mollie . . . !

MRS CARTER. Nor 'Mollie'-ing either; not after what you've done to me!

(*During the following dialogue, MRS CARTER continues taking letters from the pile and putting them on the desk. PETER helps her*)

PETER (*sharply*) *When* did I . . . (*Confused*) I mean *what* have I done?

MRS CARTER. You've broken my heart, that's all!

PETER. Mollie—Mollie . . . !

MRS CARTER (*weakening*) Yes, and not long ago it was 'Josephine, Josephine'!

PETER. But surely you don't think . . . ?

MRS CARTER. And next it'll be 'Pixie, Pixie'!

PETER. But surely you can't think I've—I've fallen for that . . . that hay-bag?

MRS CARTER. Pixie Potter?

PETER. No—the other one!

MRS CARTER. Then what were you doing playin' slap and tickles with 'er behind that screen . . .

PETER. But that was only for Pixie's benefit.

(HUMPHREY *appears cautiously at the top of the stairs*)

HUMPHREY (*to Peter*) Psst! Psst!

PETER (*turning*) Uncle!

HUMPHREY. Is it safe for me to come down there?

PETER (*with a wave towards Mrs Carter*) Well, you know Mollie better than I do!

MRS CARTER (*giggling and digging him in the ribs*) Oo! The things you say!

HUMPHREY (*descending the stairs*) Where is he? (*He moves* LC)

PETER (*moving* RC) Who?

HUMPHREY. The Bishop.

MRS CARTER. He's under the weeping willow—weepin'.

HUMPHREY (*desperately*) And that Josephine creature, where is she?

PETER. I dunno. I locked her in the potting shed, but she must've got out through the window. She isn't there now.

(HARRIETTE *appears at the top of the stairs. She has all Pixie's clothes and boots bundled up in her hands. She holds them out at arm's length. She is wearing a rubber apron over her dress*)

HARRIETTE (*firmly*) Mrs Carter!

MRS CARTER (*turning from the desk*) Now what?

HARRIETTE (*holding out the clothes*) These—*garments*—will you make them into a neat parcel. I'm sending them to Bulawayo!

MRS CARTER. What? Whose are they? (*She moves to the stairs*)

HARRIETTE (*with a glare towards Peter*) Miss Potter's!

PETER. Pixie's? (*Alarmed*) Where is she?

HARRIETTE. Locked in the bathroom. I'm giving her a bath!

PETER. But good Lord! Pixie never has a bath.

HARRIETTE (*giving the clothes to Mrs Carter*) She's having one now!

MRS CARTER (*taking the clothes and holding them at arm's length*) For cryin' out loud!

(MRS CARTER *exits into the kitchen*)

HARRIETTE (*moving upstairs*) And, Peter! When I've finished with her, I'll thank you to get that girl out of this house immediately.

PETER (*moving to the stairs*) But, Auntie—without her clothes . . . ?

HARRIETTE. She is not going to parade around the Vicarage in those dreadful things.

HUMPHREY (*muttering*) Quite dreadful!

HARRIETTE. I'd rather see her stark naked.

HUMPHREY (*innocently*) So would I!

(HARRIETTE *gives him a quick glare*)

HARRIETTE (*coming downstairs again and moving to the desk*) And, Arthur, you'd better think about what you're going to say to the Bishop! You haven't spoken to him yet, I presume?

HUMPHREY. No, not yet!

HARRIETTE (*taking a small bottle from a drawer of the desk*) I wouldn't like to be in your shoes when you do!

PETER (*noticing the bottle*) What have you got there, Auntie?

HARRIETTE (*moving to the stairs*) Aspirin. (*She puts her hand to her head*) I feel terrible. (*She goes upstairs*)

PETER. Oh, well in my room, in the chest of drawers, third drawer down, there's a bottle of . . .

HARRIETTE. Not now, there isn't!

(HARRIETTE *exits along the landing*)

HUMPHREY (*darting to the window and peeping out*) Peter! (*Desperately*) What am I going to do about the Bishop!

PETER (*moving C*) When he hands you your cards, make sure they're fully stamped.

HUMPHREY (*moving C*) I can't face him, Peter. I can't.

PETER. Oh, he's not such an eyesore as all that!

HUMPHREY (*moving to the desk; wailing*) It will be the first time we've really met—and it has to be under these distressing circumstances. (*Seeing the letters*) Oh no! Not more letters? (*Suddenly; wildly*) I can't face them! I can't (*Moving* L; *excitedly*) I can't face anyone—the Bishop—anyone! Peter, I must go!

PETER. Go where?

HUMPHREY. I must go away and hide somewhere! (*Dashing down* L) Where's my hat?

(HUMPHREY *exits down* L)

PETER (*moving towards the hall*) Hey, Uncle, take it easy!

(HUMPHREY *dashes on again, putting a hat on his head*)

HUMPHREY (*as he charges in*) Peter, didn't you say something the other day about a cave in Scotland?

PETER. No, *I* didn't; you did.

HUMPHREY. That's right!

PETER. And I said it would be spider-ridden.

HUMPHREY. I'd rather face a thousand spiders than the Bishop and all those women! (*Grabbing Peter's hand*) Good-bye, Peter! I'm going!

PETER. But where?

HUMPHREY. Scotland!

PETER. What? Look here, you can't . . .

HUMPHREY (*shaking Peter's hand wildly*) It's been nice having you stay with us, my boy!

PETER. Thanks very much, but . . .

HUMPHREY. I—I'll send you some shortbread! (*He dashes to the window*)

PETER. What about your toothbrush?

HUMPHREY (*looking out; with a yelp of panic*) Oh! Oh no! No!

PETER. Uncle . . . !

(HUMPHREY *about turns and dashes towards the hall*)

(*running to the arch and putting out his arms to stop him*) Uncle!

HUMPHREY (*wildly*) He's here!

(HUMPHREY *dashes up the stairs and off along the landing*)

PETER. But . . . (*He follows Humphrey to the stairs*)

(*The* BISHOP *enters from the window*)

(*Seeing him*) Oh Lord! (*he turns to go quickly upstairs*)

BISHOP (*loudly*) Humphrey!

PETER (*stopping with his back to the Bishop*) What did you say?

BISHOP (*firmly*) I said 'Humphrey'.

PETER. Er . . . that's what it sounded like.

BISHOP. I want a word with you!

PETER. A word?

BISHOP. Several words! You are Humphrey, are you not?

PETER. Am I! (*He takes his spectacles from his pocket and slips them on*)

BISHOP. Well, aren't you? (*He moves to the armchair*)

PETER (*turning on the stairs; mumbling*) 'It is a far, far better thing I do now than I have ever done! It is . . .'

BISHOP (*turning*) What are you jabbering about?

PETER. I was jabbering my text for Sunday morning's sermon!

BISHOP (*gaping*) Your . . . ? Can I believe my ears?

PETER (*muttering*) I dunno. You know 'em better than I do!

BISHOP. Stop mumbling, man! Have you the effrontery to tell me you are going to take next Sunday's services?

PETER (*limply*) Oh, I'm game for anything!

BISHOP. I can't believe it!

PETER. Make the effort!

BISHOP (*incredulously*) *After* putting that disgraceful advertisement in *The Times?*

PETER. Even after . . .

BISHOP. *After* all the ridicule you have brought on yourself?

PETER. Even after . . .

BISHOP. *After* the indignant letter of complaint I have received from your Church Council?

(PETER *waves a hand indicating 'Even after that!'*)

After the scathing telephone call I had from the President of the Women's Institute?

PETER (*meaning 'yes'*) Huh-huh!

BISHOP. *And* the Mothers' Union?

PETER. Huh-huh!

BISHOP. And the Darby and Joan Club?

PETER. And the Pig and Whistle Dart Club.

BISHOP (*automatically*) And the Pig and Whistle . . . (*Breaking off*) I am shocked beyond words by your conduct and your attitude of complete and utter indifference! And—(*suddenly, and angrily*)—will you kindly come down those stairs! Come here where I can get at you! (*He moves down L*)

PETER. But I don't want to be got at!

BISHOP (*facing Peter*) Will you . . . !

(PETER *comes down the stairs to* C)

(*Seething*) Humphrey—I'm speaking to you more in sorrow than in anger . . .

PETER (*with surprise*) Are you? I should've said it was the other way round!

BISHOP (*loudly*) Will you be quiet, sir!

PETER. Yes, sir.

BISHOP (*moving* L *a pace*) Have you no respect for your cloth?
PETER (*automatically*) No, sir.
BISHOP (*turning*) *What?*
PETER (*confused*) I'm so sorry! My—my . . . ?

(BISHOP *indicates Peter's attire*)

Oh, my suit! Considering what it cost. I have the *greatest* respect for it!
BISHOP. I—I . . . ! (*He is beginning to get very irate. Ominously*) Humphrey . . .
PETER. Your Worship?
BISHOP (*bellowing*) *What?*
PETER (*confused*) I beg your pardon. I'm getting confused. I was 'had up' last week for speeding.
BISHOP. You baffle me!
PETER. I bewilder myself!
BISHOP (*gaping at him*) Just how stupid can you get?
PETER. Watch me! (*He imitates a gorilla*)
BISHOP (*backing* L; *near to apoplexy*) Humphrey!
PETER. Your Highness!
BISHOP (*thundering*) *What?*
PETER. Wrong again? Never mind! I—I—I *will* get it right; give me time!
BISHOP (*crossing down* R) I wouldn't like to say you've been drinking.
PETER (*muttering*) *I* would!
BISHOP. But I can hardly believe you are yourself.
PETER (*muttering*) You can say that again!
BISHOP (*loudly*) Stop muttering, man! Are you seriously telling me that you intend taking the services next Sunday?
PETER (*moving* L *of the Bishop*) Well, you know the old saying —'The show must go on!'
BISHOP (*thundering*) *Humphrey!*
PETER. Your—your . . . (*Moving away* L, *beating his brow*) It'll come! It'll come!
BISHOP (*almost dancing with fury*) Humphrey! Humphrey!
PETER (*irritably*) What's on the flip side?
BISHOP. I—I . . . !
PETER. You must know some other names!
BISHOP (*moving* C; *gibbering*) I—I—I am incapable of speech. I . . .
PETER. That's your trouble—you're not!
BISHOP. *I will be heard!* Humphrey! It is quite obvious that you feel no shame for what you have done! Indeed, it would appear that you revel in your infamy! But I would ask you to reflect, Humphrey, on the ridicule and disgrace you have brought not only on yourself but on me, your Bishop. (*Boiling*) You have made us both laughing stocks in the eyes of the entire

country! And for that, Humphrey, I could—(*raising a clenched fist high*) I could *strike you dead at my feet!*

(MRS CARTER *rushes on from the kitchen*)

MRS CARTER (*seeing Peter*) Oh, there you . . . ! (*Moving* R *of Peter*) Will you be an angel?
PETER. Any minute now!
BISHOP (*thundering*) Leave us, woman!
MRS CARTER. But I was going to ask him if he'd . . .
BISHOP. Leave us!
PETER (*to Mrs Carter*) The Bishop would like you to leave us!
MRS CARTER (*in surprise*) 'Bishop'? (*Looking towards him*) Oh, that's what he is—one of *them!* (*She regards the Bishop curiously, then to Peter*) Funny, aren't they?

(MRS CARTER *exits to the kitchen. The* BISHOP *moves up and down, almost gibbering*)

PETER. Er—you were saying—before we were interrupted . . . ?
BISHOP (*after collapsing into the armchair*) Humphrey—(*he is very shattered*) Humphrey, you would call me a—a *just* man?
PETER (*moving* L *of the armchair; doubtfully*) 'Just'? Er, yes —just!
BISHOP. Thank you. And being just a just man—er—a just man, I am bound to hear your explanation of your conduct.
PETER. It's a very long story.
BISHOP. How long?
PETER. Well, have you read the Encyclopedia Britannica?
BISHOP (*beating the arms of the chair; at bursting point*) Humphrey, I am trying to keep calm, but I am finding it an effort.
PETER (*sympathetically*) I know; and it takes it out of you, doesn't it?
BISHOP. I repeat, I am waiting to hear your explanation of that outrageous advertisement!
PETER. Well now, the advertisement. Actually, it's all to do with oats.
BISHOP (*his eyes popping*) Oats?
PETER. Wild oats!
BISHOP. Wild oats . . . ?
PETER. Not to be confused with corn flakes.

(*The* BISHOP *gives a cross between a groan and a whinney*)

BISHOP (*broken, baffled, and near to tears*) I—I want to go home!
PETER (*dashing to the window, inserting two fingers in his mouth and giving a piercing whistle, then yelling*) Taxi!

(*The* BISHOP *leaps to his feet and moves* L *of Peter*)

BISHOP (*almost shouting*) But I won't go home!

PETER (*again giving a whistle, then waving his arm as if to say 'No taxi', then shouting*) Sorry, mate!

BISHOP. Do you think I don't see what you're trying to do? You're—you're trying to bamboozle me! (*He moves down* C)

PETER (*moving down* C *savouring the word*) Bamboozle?

BISHOP. But I will *not be* bamboozled!

PETER. I don't blame you! Sounds 'orrid!

BISHOP (*almost shouting*) Why did you put that disgusting advertisement in *The Times*? (*Louder*) And don't you dare talk to me about corn flakes!

PETER (*with 'solemnity' and dignity*) Pray be seated! (*He indicates the settee*)

BISHOP (*as he sits; suspiciously*) If this is another of your ...!

PETER (*reproachfully*) Your ... (*A beaming smile comes over his face. He sits* R *of the Bishop and taps him on the knee*) I've—got—it! I've got it! Your—*Grace!* Of course! My goodness gracious! '*Your Grace'!*

BISHOP (*firmly*) The advertisement, Humphrey!

PETER (*hurt*) Oh please, please! Let me enjoy my moment of triumph!

BISHOP (*sourly*) Do! Do! It's the last you'll have!

PETER. Kill-joy! But then—(*with a shrug of the shoulders*) that's how it's been all my life! Always when I thought happiness was within my grasp—zonk—it was snatched away!

BISHOP. What are you talking about now?

PETER. My youth.

BISHOP. Do *we have* to go as far back as that?

PETER. Well, if we were going back to *yours,* we'd need history books!

BISHOP. *What?*

PETER (*quickly going on*) When I was a callow youth—I watched all the other callow youths I knew, sowing their wild oats! But never me! Never me!

BISHOP. I should hope not!

PETER. For me, always the nose to the grindstone!

BISHOP. Commendable! Commendable!

PETER (*muttering*) But bloody boring!

BISHOP (*sharply*) *What* did you say?

PETER. Not for me the bright lights and the gaiety of dalliance with the opposite sex! I shunned them then—and as the years rolled by I shunned them even more. Oh how I shunned them!

BISHOP. Quite right!

PETER. Quite wrong! Suddenly—last week it was—I realized how empty was my life; what I was missing! Suddenly I craved the female companionship which is every man's birthright. Am I making myself clear?

BISHOP. *Very* clear!

PETER. Oh well, that's something! So—I was driven to do what I did. I advertised! (*With great appeal*) Your Grace! Can you not understand and pity me? *You*, who—after handing me my cards—will return to the bosom of your family, take your children on your knees, feel the tender embrace of the woman you love . . .

BISHOP. Confound you, sir! I shall do nothing of the kind!

PETER. Why? Are you in the dog-house?

BISHOP. I am not married, sir!

PETER. Not?

BISHOP. Not! (*Rising and moving down* R) Nor am I ever likely to be.

PETER (*rising; muttering*) *You* said it—I didn't!

BISHOP. Nor did I ever sow any wild oats in my youth.

PETER. You didn't?

BISHOP. I did not!

PETER. Not one solitary oat?

BISHOP. Not one!

PETER. What, *never*?

BISHOP. Well, *hardly ever*!

PETER (*taking up the cue, and singing—from 'H.M.S. Pinafore'*)

      Then give three cheers and one cheer more
      For the gallant captain of the . . .

BISHOP (*thundering*) Humphrey!

PETER. Your Grace?

BISHOP. You are not the only one, Humphrey, who, in his youth, turned his back on the lighter side of life, and gave himself up to serious study and constant awareness of the need for sobriety——

PETER (*quickly*) I never mentioned drink!

BISHOP (*carried away*) —Who never allowed his feet to stray from the narrow path he had been called upon to travel! Who never, by word, thought or deed——

    (MRS BARRINGTON-LOCKE'S *voice is heard booming in the hall*)

MRS BARRINGTON-LOCKE (*off*) Anyone at home?

BISHOP (*continuing his theme*) —by word, thought, or deed——

PETER (*moving* C) Oi!

BISHOP. What?

PETER. Turn it up! We've got company!

    (MRS BARRINGTON-LOCKE *sails in from down* L)

MRS BARRINGTON-LOCKE (*heartily*) Good morning, good morning, good morning!

BISHOP (*gaping at her*) Good . . . !

PETER. And three hearty 'Good morning's' to you. Er—may I introduce . . . ? (*He indicates the Bishop*)

MRS BARRINGTON-LOCKE (*gaping at the Bishop*) No!

PETER. Not? But, I do assure you—his appearance is against him. When you really know him . . .

MRS BARRINGTON-LOCKE (*with a burst*) Wally!

BISHOP (*shaken*) Winnie!

PETER. Eh?

MRS BARRINGTON-LOCKE. *Wally!*

BISHOP. *Winnie!*

PETER (*to Mrs Barrington-Locke*) Now it's your turn!

MRS BARRINGTON-LOCKE (*still gaping at the Bishop*) WALLY!

PETER (*to the Bishop*) Now yours!

BISHOP (*goggling at Mrs Barrington-Locke*) WINNIE! (*He moves* C)

PETER. Fine! (*Crossing* RC) Now, can we leave it at that?

MRS BARRINGTON-LOCKE (*incredulously, to the Bishop*) You old basket!

BISHOP (*horrified*) *Winnie!*

(MRS BARRINGTON-LOCKE *flings her arms round the Bishop and gives him several big kisses*)

MRS BARRINGTON-LOCKE. You old son-of-a-so-and-so! (*More kisses*)

BISHOP (*very embarrassed*) I—I . . . !

PETER (*politely*) Er—can I take it that you two have met before?

MRS BARRINGTON-LOCKE (*drawing back and gazing at the Bishop*) Met before? I'll say we have. (*Digging the Bishop in the ribs with her elbow*) Eh, Wally?

BISHOP. I—er—I . . .

PETER (*digging him in the ribs from the other side*) Eh, Wally?

MRS BARRINGTON-LOCKE. When he was at Cambridge: I was at Boots.

PETER. Fancy!

MRS BARRINGTON-LOCKE (*exuberantly*) Met before? Ask him about those Saturday nights at the pictures in the back row of the two-and-fourpennies!

BISHOP (*horrified*) Winnie—please . . . !

PETER (*to the Bishop; politely*) Wally, what about those Saturday nights at the pictures in the back row of the two-and-fourpenny's?

BISHOP (*glaring at Peter*) Really—I . . . !

MRS BARRINGTON-LOCKE. And ask him about that afternoon I was swimming in the river, and he ran off with my knickers.

BISHOP (*with a yelp*) Winnie!

PETER (*to the Bishop; politely*) Wally, what about that afternoon——

BISHOP. I—I . . . !

MRS BARRINGTON-LOCKE. Next time I saw 'em, they were flying from the flagpole on the City Hall!

PETER (*with tremendous mock horror*) Wal-lee!

BISHOP (*wretchedly*) It *was* Rag Week!

MRS BARRINGTON-LOCKE (*gazing happily at the Bishop*) And here you are—after all that time . . . ! (*Suddenly*) Wally! What are you doing with a dog-collar round your neck?

BISHOP. I—I went into the Church, Winnie!

MRS BARRINGTON-LOCKE (*with a wink*) Trust you to get up to *some* devilment!

BISHOP (*again with a yelp*) Winnie!

MRS BARRINGTON-LOCKE (*looking at them*) And gaiters!! Does that mean you're a Bishop?

BISHOP. I—I have that honour!

MRS BARRINGTON-LOCKE. With legs like yours, you deserve it!

BISHOP (*with a feeble laugh*) Still the same old Winnie!

MRS BARRINGTON-LOCKE. But are you still the same old Wally?

PETER (*to Mrs Barrington-Locke*) The—er—the *leopard*, you know . . . !

MRS BARRINGTON-LOCKE (*crossing down L*) *Have* you changed your spots, Wally?

BISHOP (*moving to the settee and collapsing on it*) I—er—I . . .

MRS BARRINGTON-LOCKE (*with a shrug of the shoulders*) I expect you have! I expect you sit in your Palace, looking as if butter wouldn't melt in your mouth! And how many children have you, Wally?

BISHOP. Children!

MRS BARRINGTON-LOCKE I should say, at a guess, about a dozen. You never did things by half, did you?

BISHOP (*trying to be dignified*) I have no children!

MRS BARRINGTON-LOCKE. You *haven't*?

BISHOP. I'm not married—so how could I have?

PETER (*moving C; to Mrs Barrington-Locke*) As if he didn't *know*!!

MRS BARRINGTON-LOCKE (*with great interest*) Not—*not* married!

BISHOP. No!

MRS BARRINGTON-LOCKE (*very significantly*) Oh!

BISHOP (*after looking at her; alarmed by the 'Oh!'*) But I'm very content! I—I have my television!

MRS BARRINGTON-LOCKE. Your . . . ?

BISHOP. And—er—what about you? I suppose you're . . .

MRS BARRINGTON-LOCKE (*again significantly*) I'm a widow, Wally!

BISHOP (*more alarmed*) A—a—widow?

PETER (*quietly*) A *merry* one to boot!

Mrs Barrington-Locke. Wally, are you telling me there's never been another woman in your life since—since . . .

Bishop. I have never looked at another . . .

Mrs Barrington-Locke. *What—never?*

Bishop. Well—hardly ever!

Peter (*again taking up the cue and singing*)
'Then give three cheers and one cheer more
For the gallant Captain of the . . .'

Bishop (*rising and moving* L *of Peter; barking*) Humphrey!

Peter. Oh Lord!

Mrs Barrington-Locke (*to the Bishop*) Hey! Why do you call him 'Humphrey'?

Bishop. Because he *is* Humphrey!

Mrs Barrington-Locke. He isn't, y'know!

Bishop. *Not?*

Mrs Barrington-Locke. I understood his name was Vaseline.

Peter (*murmuring*) Wintergreen.

Bishop (*thundering*) Is that true?

Peter. No!

Bishop. What isn't?

Peter. What?

Bishop. *What?*

Peter. Er—shall we start again?

Bishop (*fuming*) Is it true that you are *not* Humphrey, the incumbent of the living of St Michael and All Angels, in the Parish of Stebbington-Fawley?

Peter. Alas, it *is* true—I am *not* Humphrey, the 'whats-it' of the living of 'Who's-it and Who's-it', in the parish of 'Where-is-it Where-is-it'.

Mrs Barrington-Locke. I've told you, Wally; his name's Vaseline.

Peter (*murmuring*) Wintergreen!

Mrs Barrington-Locke. Same counter! (*To the Bishop*) He's the curate of Merton-on-Creek!

Bishop (*moving* C) I've never *heard* of it!

Peter. Don't boast! Neither have I!

Bishop (*moving* L *of Peter; almost dancing with fury*) What did you mean by saying your name was Humphrey?

Peter. I did *not* say . . .

Bishop. You *did* say.

Peter. I did not. *You* said . . .

Bishop. I did *not. I* said . . .

Peter. No you *didn't!* That's what *I* said after what *you* said!

(*The* Bishop's *mouth opens and closes several times*)

Bishop (*at last; with a whimper*) Winnie . . . !

Mrs Barrington-Locke (*coming to him*) Wally!

BISHOP (*pathetically*) One of—(*pointing to Peter*) us two is insane! Tell me, Winnie, which one is it?

MRS BARRINGTON-LOCKE (*putting an arm round him*) Now you're not to worry! They have marvellous cures these days!

BISHOP (*with a yelp*) What? (*He puts a hand to his brow*)

MRS BARRINGTON-LOCKE. Perhaps you've been seeing too much television. You know—what you want, Wally, is someone to look after you. Someone who'll take your mind off things, and—er . . .

PETER. Put it on others!

MRS BARRINGTON-LOCKE (*with a wink at Peter*) Exactly! (*Leading the Bishop to the window*) I *wonder* if I can think of anybody!

BISHOP. What . . . ? Where are you taking me?

MRS BARRINGTON-LOCKE. There's a comfy seat out here—under the weeping willow.

BISHOP. I know; I've wept there already. (*Stopping*) But I've got to see this fellow Humphrey! I've got to . . .

MRS BARRINGTON-LOCKE. *You've* got to do as you're told, my lad!

BISHOP. *What?* (*Trying to resist*) Winnie! Are you begin-. ning . . . ?

MRS BARRINGTON-LOCKE (*firmly*) I'm beginning as I mean to go on!

(MRS BARRINGTON-LOCKE *pushes the* BISHOP *firmly through the french window, then turns and grins at Peter. She then gives a 'thumbs-up' sign with one hand as she looks at Peter questioningly.* PETER, *with a jerk of the arms, gives a double 'thumbs'up' to her, together with an assuring nod of the head.* MRS BARRINGTON-LOCKE *returns the nod, grinning, and goes out through the french window.* PETER *follows quickly to the window and looks after them*)

PETER (*coming away from the window; muttering to himself*) And that's the end of The Reverend Ruddy Wintergreen! (*He quickly takes off the glasses, puts them in his pocket, ruffles his hair, moves to the stairs and quickly mounts one or two*)

(MRS CARTER *enters from the kitchen*)

MRS CARTER (*moving c; excitedly*) Are you there? Are you there?

PETER. No, I'm here! That is if it's me you . . .

MRS CARTER (*moving below the stair; excitedly*) What do you think? They've just been on about you on the wireless again. They say you're still missing!

PETER. That must've surprised you!

MRS CARTER (*suddenly*) Hey! Where are your glasses? And look at your hair!

PETER (*coming downstairs*) Dreadful, isn't it? Can't do a thing with it! Mollie—do me a favour, will you?

MRS CARTER. Course! Where's your comb?

PETER. Eh?

MRS CARTER (*putting him in the settee*) Sit down. (*Diving into Peter's breast pocket and producing a comb*) Mollie'll do it for you.

PETER. What? Oh, thanks very much! Short back and sides!

MRS CARTER. Aren't you pretending to be whatever you were pretendin' you were supposed to be any more then?

PETER. I'll work that one out, but I think the answer's No!

MRS CARTER. Oh, well in that case . . . (*She combs his hair normally*)

PETER. What's the point? Pixie's seen me—she knows I'm me! And I'm not going to roam the countryside dressed as a parson!

MRS CARTER. You know I've been thinking? P'raps if you took her in hand . . .

PETER. Took who in hand?

MRS CARTER. Pixie Potter. She's not bad-looking, really. And (*with a little sob*) I know it's noble of me to give you up to her. Course—if I was free . . . !

PETER (*romantically*) Ah, Mollie—if . . . !

MRS CARTER. But I'm not. I'm saddled with Carter, so—I must let you go.

PETER. Saddled with Pixie Potter! You're too generous!

MRS CARTER (*moving* L *and standing back; admiringly*) There!

PETER. Finished?

MRS CARTER. And you look lovely.

PETER (*rising*) Thank you, Antoine! Now—if we can just get rid of this . . . (*He undoes and slips off the collar and bib. He has a shirt with collar attached underneath*)

MRS CARTER. Give 'em to me!

PETER. Bless you, my darling (*Handing her the collar*) Now into my emergency disguise outfit and I'm off!

MRS CARTER (*with a little howl*) Ooh, my lovely! (*She rushes involuntarily into his arms*)

(*The* PHOTOGRAPHER *appears at the french window*)

PHOTOGRAPHER. 'Scuse me!

(PETER, *still with arms round Mrs Carter, turns*)

PETER. What . . . ?

PHOTOGRAPHER (*recognizing him; with a yelp*) Blimey! 'Venture Man'! (*Quickly raising his camera*) Hold it! (*He clicks the camera*)

PETER. Hey!

PHOTOGRAPHER (*grinning*) Thanks, Peter! You're a pal! What a turn-up for the Final Editions!

(*The* PHOTOGRAPHER *dashes off through the french window*)

PETER (*dashing to the window*) Hey! Just a minute!
MRS CARTER. Did he take us both?
PETER. He did, blast him!
MRS CARTER (*aghast*) In each others' arms? Oh my . . . !
(*Moving towards the window*) Gawd help us if Carter sees it!
Hey! Come back! Come back!

(MRS CARTER *exits through the french window.* PETER *goes quickly to the stairs.* HUMPHREY *appears on the landing. He is now wearing Peter's leather jacket from Act One, wig, beard, sunglasses, and a bright scarf hiding his dog-collar. He has Peter's guitar slung over his shoulder*)

PETER (*seeing him*) What the . . . ? (*He backs away from the stairs*)

(HUMPHREY *quickly brings up the guitar as Peter did on his first entrance—strums as he sings in an uncertain voice:* 'Yes! Yes! Yes!'

PETER. What?
HUMPHREY (*repeating*) Yes! Yes! Yes!
PETER. For heaven's sake . . . !
HUMPHREY. You've no idea *who* I am, have you, Peter?
PETER. Uncle, have you gone . . . ?
HUMPHREY. No, but I'm going! (*Suddenly*) How did you know it was me? (*He comes downstairs, removing the sunglasses*)
PETER. Uncle, you can't go to Scotland looking like that!
HUMPHREY (*moving* C) Why not, my boy?
PETER. They'll never let you in! (*He moves down* L)
HUMPHREY (*very pleased with himself*) I think this costume makes me look rather—what is the expression—'with it!'
PETER (*firmly*) Whether it does or it doesn't, you're going *without* it!
HUMPHREY (*raising the guitar again and strumming as he sings and stamps*)
             'I know just what I'm facin'
             It's me'll do the chasin'!'

PETER. Uncle!
HUMPHREY (*suddenly using a raucous voice*) Aw, belt up!
PETER. *What?*
HUMPHREY. Keep it cool, baby!
PETER (*staggered*) Uncle!
HUMPHREY (*in his own voice*) You see, I know all the expressions! Well, good-bye, my boy! (*Moving towards the window*)

Now let me think—Scotland! Do I take the high road or the low?

PETER (*rushing across to him and snatching the wig and beard off*) Sorry, Uncle! No can do! *I* want these! I'm going to Wales!

HUMPHREY (*wildly*) But, Peter . . .

(HARRIETTE *appears on the landing*)

HARRIETTE. Arthur!

HUMPHREY. Oh my goodness, Harriette!

HARRIETTE. What are you doing in that ridiculous jacket? Take it off at once!

HUMPHREY. But—Harriette . . .

HARRIETTE. And get rid of that banjo! What on earth will Pixie think?

(HUMPHREY *removes the guitar, jacket and scarf*)

PETER. Pixie?

HARRIETTE (*ignoring him, and speaking off along the landing*) Now, come along, my dear! Don't be shy!

PETER (*moving up* RC) Hey! What . . . ?

HARRIETTE (*coming downstairs*) Be nice to her, Peter.

PETER. To who?

HARRIETTE. Pixie. You too, Arthur!

PETER. I'm off! (*He makes as if to go through the window*)

HARRIETTE. You will stay where you are! (*Moving below the settee*) You too, Arthur! You see she hasn't any clothes . . .

PETER. *What?*

HUMPHREY (*innocently*) Oh, *I'll* stay!

HARRIETTE. *Arthur!*

(PIXIE *now appears on the landing. She is completely transformed. Her face is devoid of any make-up, and positively glitters. Her hair is pulled back and tied with a red bow on top, and hangs down her back. She wears an old-fashioned, puffed-sleeve dress, white socks and shoes, and her whole appearance suggests Alice in 'Alice in Wonderland'*)

PETER (*with a yelp*) Jeepers Creepers!

(PIXIE *comes demurely down the stairs*) ON

HARRIETTE. It's a dress that should have gone to Bulawayo.

PETER (*muttering*) My God, it should! (*Then as he continues to look at her*) Pixie—is it really you?

PIXIE (*with a gulp*) Yes, Peter!

PETER (*gaping*) But, Pixie—you look—human! You look—beautiful!

PIXIE (*with a little sob*) Peter! (*She rushes into his arms*)

PETER. And your hair— it smells of . . .

HARRIETTE. Carbolic soap!

PETER (*gaping at Pixie, holding her so he can see her fully*) I never realized you could look so . . . (*Overcome*) Oh hell!

HARRIETTE. Peter!

PETER (*still overcome*) Oh my goodness! Oh my . . . Pixie! (*He takes her into his arms again quickly and kisses her*)

HUMPHREY (*stepping forward*) Ahem!

HARRIETTE (*sharply*) Arthur! What are you doing?

HUMPHREY. Waiting *my* turn!

PIXIE (*coming out of the embrace; in a coy little voice*) I—I've got my man! I've got my man! (*Rushing into Peter's arms again*) Pe-ter!

(MRS CARTER *runs in from the french windows*)

MRS CARTER (*as she comes in*) Quick! Quick! (*Seeing Peter and Pixie in embrace; with a sob*) Oooh!

HARRIETTE. What is it, Mrs Carter?

MRS CARTER (*pulling herself together*) That photographer chap, he's let it out that—(*to Peter*) that *you're* up here! All the women in the village are coming up the drive!

HARRIETTE. Oh no!

MRS CARTER (*to Peter*) And *Carter's* leading 'em!

PETER. *What?*

HARRIETTE (*quickly*) Peter! Lock the front door!

(PETER *dashes off down* L. PIXIE *runs* L)

(*Moving up* RC) Arthur! The french window!

HUMPHREY (*dashing to the window*) Yes, Harriette! (*At the window*) Oh! Oh! Oh! (*He backs down* C)

HARRIETTE. What . . . ?

(*The* BISHOP *and* MRS BARRINGTON-LOCKE *appear at the window*)

BISHOP (*as they come in*) But, Winnie, I assure you I haven't been lonely! I've had my television!

MRS BARRINGTON-LOCKE. But not in *bed*, surely? I won't stand for that, Wally! (*She moves to the desk*)

HARRIETTE. Winifred . . . !

BISHOP (*seeing Humphrey*) Aaah! (*Moving* C) Humphrey!

HUMPHREY (*mumbling*) My Lord . . . ! (*He moves* C)

BISHOP (*beginning to boil*) So we meet at last, eh!

HUMPHREY. My Lord—Your Grace . . .

BISHOP (*thundering*) You know why I'm here, don't you? I want a word with you!

HUMPHREY. My Lord, I do assure you it was all a mistake—and, in any case I've changed my mind—I don't *want* to get married!

BISHOP. According to the advertisement you never *did*!

HARRIETTE (*rushing forward* R *of the Bishop*) Forgive me,

Your Grace, but could we delay your talk with my brother just
for now. You see . . .

(*There is the sound of women's loud voices off up* R *and
down* L)

BISHOP. I do not see! But I intend to! I . . . (*He breaks off*)
What is all that noise outside?
HUMPHREY. Women! Dozens of them!
BISHOP. Clients of *yours*, I suppose!
HARRIETTE. No, no, Your Grace! They're after our nephew!
BISHOP. Your . . . ?
HARRIETTE. Yes, you see, he—he appears on television. He's
very popular and . . .
BISHOP (*interested at once*) Oh?
HARRIETTE. You may have heard of him. Peter——
HUMPHREY. —'Venture Man'——
HARRIETTE. —Graham.
BISHOP (*with a yelp*) *What?*

(*The noise of women is getting nearer*)

HARRIETTE (*in alarm*) Those women! Arthur . . . ! The french
windows! Close them! Lock them!
HUMPHREY. Yes, Harriette!

(HUMPHREY *dashes to the window, closes and locks it. Just
as he does so,* JOSEPHINE *appears outside and flattens herself
up against the window*)

JOSEPHINE (*outside the window; loudly*) Beloved!

(HUMPHREY, *with a yelp of alarm, moves* C)

BISHOP (*goggling*) 'Venture Man'! *'Venture Man'* your—*your*
nephew! I can't believe . . . ! (*To Humphrey*) Humphrey!
HUMPHREY (*turning, in trepidation*) Your Grace . . . ?
BISHOP (*his whole attitude turning to respect and awe*) My
dear Humphrey . . . !
HUMPHREY (*tremulously*) My dear Bishop . . .
BISHOP (*taking his hand*) My *very* dear Humphrey!
HUMPHREY (*not knowing what it is all about; shaking the
Bishop's hand*) My *very* dear Bishop!
BISHOP. 'Venture Man'—*your* nephew . . . !
HUMPHREY. Yes, Your Grace!
BISHOP (*still with awe*) Amazing! Incredible! My favourite
programme! My favourite star! My . . .

(PETER *dashes in down* L. *The* BISHOP *goggles at him. The
noise outside increases. Women's voices can be heard shouting 'Venture Man!', 'Peter!', 'We want Peter!', etc.*)

PETER (*running in to* LC) Uncle, there are women all over the
place—hundreds of 'em! I've got to hide! I've got to . . .

BISHOP (*finding his voice*) It is!
PETER (*pulled up with a jerk*) What?
BISHOP. It is! It's him! He! (*Rushing across to Peter*) 'Venture Man'! (*He suddenly gives a long moan, a spin, and does a 'Mrs Carter' faint into Peter's arms*)
PETER (*almost collapsing; yelling*) Help!

HUMPHREY *rushes behind Peter, supporting him with his hands on Peter's back, as—*

the CURTAIN *falls*

FIRST CALL—*Entire cast lined up*

SECOND CALL—*Entire cast lined up. All sing 'I'll Get My Man', with clapping and stamping.*

FURNITURE AND PROPERTY LIST

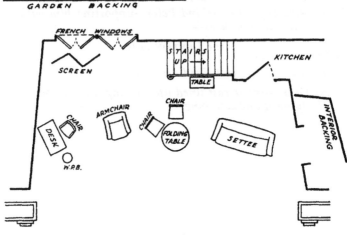

ACT I

On stage—Settee (LC). *On it:* cushions

Armchair (RC). *On it:* cushion

Gate-legged table (C). *On it:* large white cloth, 2 plates, 2 cups, 2 saucers, dish, knives, teaspoons, table napkins, small milk jug, barley water, sugar caster, copies of *Daily Mail* and *The Times*

Desk (R) *On it:* writing materials, pad, telephone, book. *In drawer:* small bottle

Wooden swivel desk-chair

Occasional table (up C). *On it:* bowl of flowers, ornaments, large photograph of 'Peter'

2 small chairs (above and R of table C)

Large moveable screen (up R)

Metal wastepaper-basket (below desk)

Carpet

Mat (under desk)

Window curtains

Off stage—Plate with 2 sausages (MRS CARTER)

Duster (MRS CARTER)

Tray with small pot of coffee, toast rack with 4 Ryvita-type biscuits, small bowl in which is what appears to be a bundle of straw (MRS CARTER)

Daily Mirror (MRS CARTER)

Tray (MRS CARTER)

Hoover (MRS CARTER)

Bundle of clothes (HARRIETTE)

Guitar (PETER)

Canvas hold-all (PETER)

88

Personal—MRS BARRINGTON-LOCKE: handbag with opened envelope and
          letter; horn-rimmed glasses; watch
          HARRIETTE: watch
          PETER: dark glasses; wig; false beard

ACT II
SCENE 1

Strike—Tablecloth

Set—*Daily Mail* on desk
     The Times on desk
     Piece of paper under desk mat

Off stage—Shears (HUMPHREY)
           Tray set for large breakfast for one (MRS CARTER)
           Mailbag crammed with letters, some done up in bundles (MRS
           CARTER)
           Tray with cup of coffee (MRS CARTER)
           Press camera (PHOTOGRAPHER)

Personal—HUMPHREY: handkerchief
          PETER: horn-rimmed spectacles

SCENE 2

Set—Letters on and around desk
     Wheelbarrow loaded with letters outside window (optional)
     Newspaper on desk

Off stage—Used breakfast tray (HARRIETTE)
           Newspaper (HARRIETTE)
           Newspaper (PETER)
           Parasol, handbag, cakebox containing stones painted to resemble
           rock buns (JOSEPHINE)
           Letter without envelope (HUMPHREY)
           Folded newspaper (PIXIE)

Personal—HUMPHREY: Peter's dark glasses

ACT III

Off stage—Mailbag full of loose and bundled letters (BISHOP)
           Pixie's Act II clothes in bundle (HARRIETTE)
           Press camera (PHOTOGRAPHER)
           Peter's jacket, wig, beard, dark glasses, guitar (HUMPHREY)

Personal—BISHOP: handkerchief
          HARRIETTE: rubber apron
          PETER: spectacles; comb

LIGHTING PLOT

Property fittings required—as desired for dressing only

Interior. A living-room. The same scene throughout
THE APPARENT SOURCE OF LIGHT is a large french window up RC
THE MAIN ACTING AREAS are R, up RC, down RC, C, LC, down L

ACT I Morning
To open: Effect of bright spring morning
No cues
ACT II SCENE 1 Morning
To open: As previous act
No cues
ACT II SCENE 2 Morning
To open: As previous scene
No cues
ACT III Morning
To open: As previous act
No cues

EFFECTS PLOT

ACT I

Cue 1   MRS CARTER: 'I'm only telling you'   (page 16)
Telephone rings

ACT II
SCENE 1

Cue 2   MRS CARTER: '. . . do 'is back, bless 'im'   (page 30)
Door bell rings

Cue 3   MRS BARRINGTON-LOCKE: '. . . on in this house?'   (page 34)
Telephone rings

Cue 4   HARRIETTE: 'In what, man, what?'   (page 42)
Door bell rings

Cue 5   HUMPHREY drinks coffee   (page 43)
Telephone rings

SCENE 2

Cue 6   On CURTAIN up   (page 47)
Telephone and door bell ring

Cue 7   MRS CARTER exits   (page 47)
Telephone rings

Cue 8   PETER: 'Waxy Lax'   (page 52)
Telephone rings

Cue 9   JOSEPHINE: 'Tonight!'   (page 59)
Door bell rings

Cue 10   HUMPHREY: '. . . a return ticket?'   (page 59)
Door bell rings

Cue 11   HUMPHREY: '. . . thinking I didn't!'   (page 59)
Door bell rings

Cue 12   PIXIE: 'I gotta!'   (page 61)
Door bell rings

Cue 13   PIXIE: 'I heard him!'   (page 62)
Door bell rings

Cue 14   MRS CARTER: 'My Gawd! 'Er!'   (page 62)
Door bell rings

ACT III

Cue 15   BISHOP: 'May I ask . . . ?'   (page 64)
Door bell rings

Cue 16   PETER and JOSEPHINE exit   (page 64)
Door bell rings

Cue 17   MRS CARTER exits   (page 64)
Door bell rings

Cue 18   MRS CARTER: '. . . pass the time'   (page 67)
Telephone rings

Lightning Source UK Ltd.
Milton Keynes UK
UKOW06f1548251116
288574UK00001B/36/P